Cheerleading
and Song Leading

also by RON HUMPHREY

Juggling for Fun and Entertainment

Cheerleading and Song Leading

by Marylou and Ron Humphrey

Charles E. Tuttle Company

RUTLAND · VERMONT : TOKYO · JAPAN

REPRESENTATIVES
For Continental Europe
BOXERBOOKS, INC., *Zurich*
For the British Isles
PRENTICE-HALL INTERNATIONAL, INC., *London*
For Australasia
PAUL FLESCH & CO., PTY. LTD., *Melbourne*
For Canada
M. G. HURTIG, LTD., *Edmonton*

Published by the Charles E. Tuttle Company, Inc.
of Rutland, Vermont & Tokyo, Japan
with editorial offices at
Suido 1-chome, 2–6, Bunkyo-ku, Tokyo

Copyright in Japan, 1970
by Charles E. Tuttle Company, Inc.

Library of Congress Catalog Card No. 73-104199
International Standard Book No. 0-8048 0088-X

First printing, 1970

PRINTED IN JAPAN

Dedication

This book is dedicated to those who have done so much to promote and improve cheerleading and song leading . . . and to the directors and instructors of the many fine clinics and camps, including among others: Sylvia Blair, Oregon; L. K. Herkimer, Texas; Chet Jones, Oregon; Duke Miller, Arizona; Robert Olmstead, California; Smith-Walbridge, Indiana, and the thousands of devoted and enthusiastic squad advisers throughout North America.

Table of Contents

List of Illustrations

Also, line drawings in the text, by Hide Doki

Introduction

Since sports events are enjoying a fast-growing popularity, the directing of the cheering efforts of the spectators has become a big and important job that requires study, training, and practice.

You, the cheerleader or song leader, are the link between the spectators and the team. You are an active participant who can exert a greater influence on the actual outcome of the game than you probably realize.

You have important responsibilities. You create the mood and attitude of your student body at athletic contests, and you can develop, or destroy, sportsmanship at your school.

If you want to be an effective leader, you must accomplish two goals. First, you must convey to the team the feeling that the rooters are 100 percent behind them 100 percent of the time. Second, you should make the cheering section feel that they play an active, vital role in the playing of the game. If you succeed at both, credit yourself with a winning effort, regardless of the outcome of the game.

You will need the respect, admiration, loyalty, and, above all, the cooperation of the fans in order to do your job well. This will require sacrifices on your part. It is going to take time, planning, and energy, but the rewards are many. Here are just a few that you can look forward to: popularity and prestige; the chance to develop and display your ideas; the chance to develop and demonstrate your ability; leadership training and practice in organizing group efforts; the pleasure of participation in a worthwhile activity; and a chance to help your school and student body.

Cheerleading and Song Leading assumes that you want to do the best possible job for yourself and your school. Its purpose is to describe the general responsibilities of your position and give you advice and guidance in developing your style and technique. It can help you become a popular and remembered leader at your school.

A note to cheerleaders: This book does not contain a collection of finished cheers ready for use. Such cheers can be obtained at clinics and camps or through special publications. Ready-made cheers are subject to becoming outdated quickly and, in many cases, words and phrases having a special meaning in one part of the country may be meaningless elsewhere. But more importantly, ready-made cheers encourage you to imitate rather than create. The purpose of this book is to help you become an outstanding cheerleader, well qualified to prepare refreshing, original cheers that will build a reputation for your school.

HOW TO USE THIS BOOK

Are You Already on the Cheerleading Squad or Interested in Cheerleading?

You will find helpful information in Parts II, III, and IV.

Are You the Captain of the Cheerleading Squad?

There is information of particular interest to you in Chapters 3, 4, 5, and 10.

Are You Interested in Song Leading and Pom Poms?*

Part V is especially for you. You will also find helpful information in Chapters 2, 9, and 11.

Are You Planning to Try Out for a Squad?

Read the next page and then refer back to the above for the sections that apply to your interests. If you are still not

---

* Pom pom (pompon) has become the accepted term for these ornaments by the many people engaged in song-leading activities.

sure whether you will prefer cheerleading or song leading, read the whole book and then decide.

Are You an Adviser or a Pep Club Member?

You will find helpful information in Chapter 5 and Part III.

CHEERLEADING OR SONG LEADING?

The cheerleading and song-leading responsibilities are assigned to two different units at many schools. Here is a brief discussion of the functions of each to help you decide which activity is for you.

Cheerleading

Both boys and girls make good cheerleaders. Many schools prefer boys, but combination boy-girl teams and all-girl teams are popular, too.

Purpose of Cheerleaders. The cheerleaders' main job is to control and direct the students. They develop the cheer routines and lead the students in cheering. They are often responsible for the pep rallies.

Desired Qualities. Cheerleading candidates are expected to show leadership ability, public-speaking ability, a basic knowledge of game rules, and they should have coordination, a good sense of rhythm, physical strength, and agility.

Song Leading

Song leaders are always girls. Those chosen are usually among the most attractive and popular students at their school.

Purpose of Song Leaders. The song leaders' primary purpose is to perform during the singing of school songs and to entertain the students with special routines during pauses in game activity.

Desired Qualities. Song leaders should be attractive, popular, graceful, have a good feeling for rhythm, and be able to learn new dance steps quickly.

Qualities Expected in Both Cheerleaders and Song Leaders

In addition to the specific qualities mentioned, student leaders are expected to be prompt, dependable, loyal to their

school, able to put duty ahead of personal desires, cooperative, enthusiastic about sports, good students, and good
sports.

I

You as a Student Leader

1

Confidence in Yourself

How to Acquire It

CONFIDENCE FOR THE TRYOUT

Tryouts are held for one reason: to determine the candidates who will make the best cheerleaders and song leaders. The judges will be looking for a number of qualities and abilities but one of the most important is self-confidence.

Nearly everyone has some self-confidence. Just by showing interest in trying out indicates that you are confident that you have something to offer your school as a student leader.

Self-confidence means simply that you believe in yourself and your abilities. You are confident that, with training and practice, you will be a good cheerleader or song leader. If you lack self-confidence, you will find it surprisingly easy to acquire.

The first step is to get all the information you can on cheerleading. This book will get you started. Then talk to other cheerleaders and get their ideas and suggestions. Attend cheerleading camps and clinics in your area.

The next step is practice. The better you know the routines you will use for the tryout, the more confidence you will have.

For tryout purposes, you will be better off with a couple of routines that you can do well rather than a number of routines that are not perfected. Determine how many you will be asked to perform for the tryout and then select the ones you do best. Practice them until you can do them without thinking.

Once you start learning your routines, get a small group to watch you practice. Start with your family or a few friends. Ask them to watch you and make suggestions for improvement. While giving you ideas, they will also give you practice at working in front of others. Sometimes your friends may become so interested that they will want to join you and try out as a team. Many cheerleading squads were started this way. But whether you try out as a team or alone, the more practice you have in public, the more confident you will be at the tryout.

CONFIDENCE AS A CHEERLEADER

Every cheerleader must show self-confidence all the time— at school, at rallies, and at games. You cannot do a good job or expect the students to yell their best if you are not sure of yourself. They will have confidence in you if you are organized and always know what is coming next. Plan your rallies in advance so that everyone involved knows what they are to do. Plan which yells you will use at the game and go through the new ones yourself shortly before the game. At the game, as soon as you finish one cheer, start planning the next. Since this will depend on the situation, you will have to follow the game closely.

Learn the rules and signals the officials use. Read the newspapers to see what sportswriters say about your team and your opponents. Then watch the game without becoming so emotionally involved that you cannot do a good job of cheerleading. If you understand the game and what is happening, you will not ask for inappropriate cheers.

No matter how much you practice, you may still make an occasional mistake while leading a cheer. Keep right on going as though nothing had happened. If you stop or laugh, you will attract attention to the error. But if you keep going, many may not be aware of your mistake.

CONFIDENCE ON A MICROPHONE

All cheerleaders should be able to speak over a microphone. The cheerleaders help teach yells at the rallies and sometimes announce them at the games.

The ability to speak clearly and naturally over a microphone comes with practice. Ask your adviser to arrange for you to practice with a microphone when the auditorium is not in use. When speaking to a large group, imagine that you are talking to just one person, such as a close friend. Forget that others are in the room and talk to this "person." If you do this well, you can make everyone feel that you are talking to them personally.

See that your microphone is in the right position for you. Adjust it to the proper height before you start to talk. Stand up straight with your feet together. If your hands get in the way, hold them behind your back. If you use notes, refer to them but do not read them. If you memorize what you are going to say word for word, it may sound unnatural and there is always the chance that you may forget. Just have in mind what you want to say, and say it. Do not shout into the microphone. People want to be talked to; they do not like to be shouted at. If your normal speaking voice is very soft, the operator will increase the volume.

CONFIDENCE IN YOU

You know all of your routines well and have practiced them thoroughly. You know that your cheering section can follow you. You know that you have planned every possible detail. You understand your job and you want to do the best you can. And you will.

2

Your Personal Popularity

At School and at the Games

SEEING YOURSELF AS OTHERS SEE YOU

Here is a list of personal characteristics on which you are going to be rated by other students and school officials. This will be done on a continuing basis all year around, whether you are aware of it or not. To see yourself as others see you, look over the list and rate yourself.

1. Do you stay healthy and radiate youthful vigor and enthusiasm? You are a part of the athletic team and their rules for training should apply to you.

2. Do you achieve respect as a leader by earning it, or by throwing your weight around?

3. Do you act in a responsible adult way? Try to anticipate problems and help solve them impartially.

4. Are you a good sport? Since you are in the public eye most of the time, you should save emotional displays for moments of privacy.

5. Do you keep your uniform spotlessly clean and in good condition?

6. Are you a leader in other ways? You should feel a responsibility to set a good example in everything you do, including your studies.

7. Do you have the respect of other student leaders and school officials through a willingness to cooperate with them?

YOUR PUBLIC IMAGE AT THE GAME

When you are not performing, concentrate on the game. Avoid the tendency to practice parts of routines or to wander over to the cheering section to talk with friends. If you concentrate on the game and your job, you will not be tempted to amuse yourself in other ways.

Between performances, keep out of the spectators' line of vision. If you sit down on the sidelines, do so in proper order so each will be in his place when you stand to perform the next cheer. The time for yells and songs is always short; part of it should not be wasted in getting organized.

Watch your personal actions during pauses. If you think of yourself as a performer on a stage the entire time you are at the game, you will be less likely to do anything you might be ashamed of later. You have seen what others look like when they stand and sit in awkward positions, chew gum, and adjust their hair and clothing. You should also resist the temptation to joke with other squad members, or to clown around when things get boring.

Always yell the cheers and sing the songs with the students. If you must concentrate so hard on the routine that you forget to say the words, you need more practice.

When you are leading a cheer or a song, look up at the cheering section. Tip your head up so that you are looking at an area about halfway up in the stands. If you do this, you will appear to be looking at the entire section. If you look straight ahead, it will seem as if you are interested in only the front rows.

If one of the spectators aims an insulting remark or joke at you, do not take it seriously unless you can relate it to something you might be doing wrong. Think over the way you are doing the cheers or songs. If the joke helps you uncover some problem, consider it to be constructive criticism. If the heckler is merely trying to get you to notice him, smile in his direction but do not pay any particular attention to him.

One of the jobs of squad captains is to relate the cheering to the action of the game. This means they should learn the basic rules of the game and follow the plays. They should not get so emotionally involved in the game that they forget their obligation to the students. If they do, they risk losing their job to other squad members or to students eager to start up their own yells.

YOUR PUBLIC IMAGE AT SCHOOL

You are the same person to your fellow students whether you are talking to them between classes or directing them at games and rallies. A popular cheerleader or song leader is expected to be peppy and enthusiastic all the time. An enthusiastic approach to everything should be natural for you. If you enjoy being on the squad, let it show when you perform and your enthusiasm will spread to others.

Watch your social circle. If you allow yourself to become drawn into a small, exclusive group, you will lose contact with many of the students whose support you need. Your social circle should be drawn from the entire student body. Learn the names of as many students and teachers as you can. Everyone likes the sound of his own name, so let people hear their names when you greet them. You probably will not get to know each student in your school, yet you will want to get the support of as many as you can. The students who do not know you personally will support you if they like the way you talk and act.

Popular students usually make good cheerleaders because they have many friends who support them. They are well-liked individuals who are constantly making new friends.

A friendly personality is easy to develop if you are sincerely interested in people and make an honest effort to get along with them *all the time*.

Popular students are liked by many different types of people. They are careful not to offend those who disapprove of extremes in dress and behavior.

Popular students know how to listen as well as talk. Ask people for their ideas and suggestions and they will be flattered that you thought their opinions important. Listen to what they have to say (you do not have to agree) and they will be more willing to listen to you. If you show that you are aware of the interests of others, they will be considerate of your ideas and opinions.

HOW TO BE POPULAR WITH THE COACHES AND TEAM

Players and coaches usually express two general complaints about cheerleaders:

1. The cheers are sometimes poorly timed and interfere with the game. (As examples, they list loud yells at football games while the team is huddling and trying to hear the instructions; and cheerleaders who are still out on the basketball floor when play is ready to resume.)

2. Cheers sometimes give recognition to one player, overlooking the importance of team effort and coaching. (An example is "Yea, Jones!" after he catches a touchdown pass.)

You can easily avoid these mistakes with a little bit of thought and planning. Choose cheers that fit the length of time you have. If, by accident, you are still on the floor when play is ready to resume, stop the yell or routine and get out of the way immediately. Time your yells so that the crowd gives an extra "Fight!" just when the team needs it most. Recognize the whole team and the coaching staff in your yells. Let them know that the student body is proud of their efforts, win or lose.

Cooperate with the coaches and players and ask them for suggestions and opinions. If they are pleased with your work, they will be happy to cooperate with you at the rallies and games.

Your overall popularity with the team and coaches is also going to be influenced by your ability to get the student body to attend and participate in the games and rallies.

HOW TO BE A POPULAR LEADER

You will do a better job as cheerleader for your school if you are an admired and respected student leader. But notice that the word is *leader*, not *boss*. A boss *orders* people to do things, but a leader *inspires* people to action.

Leaders are people who are popular and have ideas. They

are not necessarily the smartest, the best looking, or the hardest working. They set good examples in their appearance, behavior, and their approach to each job. They are on time for rehearsals and meetings, and they can be counted on to support fair decisions that benefit everyone. They know how to get people to get along with one another and work out compromises when problems occur.

Leaders recognize good ideas presented by others and use them, giving credit where it is due. They know how to make others feel important without lowering themselves. Their importance is self-evident; they do not have to blow their own horn.

A good student leader will be regarded by the student body as a person who takes his responsibilities seriously. If you can cause the students and teachers to regard you as a student leader, you will have their support as a cheerleader.

You can achieve this by practicing leadership. Volunteer for school, class, or club projects and then show interest, dependability, and maturity so that you will be chosen as project leader or assistant chairman. Whenever you serve as a leader, you gain additional leadership experience and you cause others to think of you as a leader.

LOOK LIKE A LEADER

Certain people look like leaders. Their appearance indicates they take pride in their work and that they enjoy having others come to them for advice. As you get to know them better, their image of a leader becomes stronger because of their sincerity, efficiency, and ability to do things right and to finish what they start.

If you are going to work at being a student leader, consider it a full-time job. Assume that you are always in the public eye, and take pride in your personal appearance. Since leaders must appeal to a wide variety of people, you should avoid extremes in your manner of dress. Be neat, clean, and always look organized.

THE SECRET OF LEADERSHIP

Have you ever wondered how student leaders could be active in so many projects yet still get good grades and have free time? Here is their secret: They know that *effective leaders delegate the time-consuming jobs to others.*

The job of a leader is to advise and supervise. You can be a leader to several groups with the same amount of time and energy that it takes to be a follower in one.

Each leader's degree of success depends on his ability to delegate jobs and responsibilities wisely. A good leader knows which jobs he can delegate, who he can delegate them to, and which jobs he must do himself. A leader who ends up doing all the jobs himself is a poor leader.

When people choose leaders, they look for someone they think will help make the efforts of the group more enjoyable and more effective. They want someone who will be a worthy representative and bring credit to their organization or project. They will look for someone who acts like a leader. If you act like a follower, you will not be recognized as a leader.

Good leaders first learn to be good followers. While they are followers, they demonstrate dependability, initiative, and the ability to organize. When the first leadership opportunity comes along, no matter how small or unimportant, they volunteer for the job.

Leadership ability can become one of your most valued qualities, not only for cheerleading but for your future as well. It is easily obtained if you set a definite plan for working toward it.

IF YOU ARE PLANNING TO TRY OUT

All schools have their own methods for choosing cheerleaders. While methods may vary, the judges will rate you on certain general qualities. Here they are:

Your Personal Appearance
1. Good physical proportions. Not overweight or underweight.
2. Neat in appearance and personal habits.

Your Personality Qualities
1. Prompt and dependable.
2. Loyal to the school and able to put duty above personal desires.
3. A good sport and cooperative.
4. Good scholastic standing.

Your Routines
1. Suitable and in good taste.
2. High in spectator appeal.
3. Original.

The Way You Do Your Routines
1. Personality projection.
2. Self-confidence and poise.
3. Rhythm and timing.
4. Coordination of arm and leg movements with words.
5. Voice quality and microphone ability.
6. Grace and variety of jumps.
7. Pep and enthusiasm.
8. Precision.

Get all the information you can about the tryout ahead of time. Determine what is expected of you so that you will be completely prepared. This will also impress those in charge of the tryout that you have a sincere interest in doing a good job, one of the primary qualities of a good cheerleader.

3

Training a Cheering Section

Getting Them to Cheer with You

HOW DO YOU MAKE THE STUDENTS YELL?

You *don't*. You cannot make them do anything if they are not in the mood. They go to games because they want excitement and they want to encourage their team. If there are not any cheerleaders, they will yell anyway. However, they know that unorganized yelling is not as effective as well-planned cheers. Since they cannot cheer without a leader, they will follow the cheerleaders. So you *don't* have to make them yell. You just tell them what to say and when. *It's* that simple.

Certain cheering sections, however, do a better job of supporting their team than others. These have been trained by their cheerleaders to start and stop together, to make their yells sharp, crisp, clear, and easily heard by the team. They have been trained to watch for special motions that have special meanings. A little bit of training has turned ordinary cheering sections into rooters that are admired by their team and envied by other schools. Here is how it is done:

USE THE RALLY AS YOUR PRACTICE SESSION

Never teach new yells during the game. You will be laughed at, the yells probably will not work, and you will embarrass your team and cheering section. Everyone makes mistakes while they are learning. Use the rally as your training session and make your mistakes there, not at the game.

Explain any special motions that you use, such as a "cut-off" that means you want silence. Demonstrate and teach your new yells at the rally. Then give the new cheer a final rehearsal before the game starts.

HOW TO KEEP THE ATTENTION OF THE CHEERING SECTION

The attention of your cheering section will be on the game while play is in progress. During a cheer, it must be on the cheerleaders. This means you should never start a cheer during a play.

At the rallies, ask the students to watch you carefully during each yell. Tell them you are going to show them when to start and stop, how fast to yell and how loud. You are going to show how long they should pause between words and when. If they do not watch you, they are going to make embarrassing mistakes.

A good way to encourage them to watch you is for you to watch them throughout the yell. Your eyes should be on the cheering section from the moment you announce the yell until you end it. If you turn sideways during a cheer, keep your head turned toward the cheering section. Do not turn your back on the rooters. Look at them, smile at them, and you will charm them into watching and following you.

Follow the game and relate your cheers to the action. Decide on the next cheer before you get up for it. Do not waste time, and you will keep the confidence of the cheering section.

At football games announce each cheer a play early, if possible. During the huddle, the cheerleader captain might announce, "After the next play, we will give a FIGHT!" Immediately following the play, all cheerleaders announce it again. This gives the cheering section a chance to think about the cheer that is coming up and keeps them alert.

HOW TO START A CHEER

Every cheer should have a "click-off," or starting signal. This can be either a couple of words, such as, "Ready, Hit It!" or a question by the cheerleaders and an answer from the students. A popular one is, "All Set? YOU BET!"

They should be short, snappy, and easily understood by the students. Good starting signals will do three things for you:

1. Get everybody started on the first word. Without a starting signal, it is difficult to tell when the cheerleaders want the yell to begin. To avoid the embarrassment of starting too soon, they will wait until the cheer is well under way to join in. When this happens, the first part of the yell is not even heard by the team.

You will always find students who will not join a yell if it gets started without them. As a result, they never yell with the group. But if you can get everyone to start with you through the use of a starting signal, they will cheer louder and stay with you to the end. The first word following the starting signal should be easy to say and given with a big motion.

2. Determine how fast to yell. Your starting signal can tell the cheering section how fast you want them to yell the words. It is simple. The starting signal is given in the same rhythm as the yell is to be done. When the cheerleaders give the starting signal, it tells the cheering section that the yell that follows is to be done in the same tempo.

3. Alert everyone. No matter how many times you announce a yell there will always be some students who did not pay attention. They will not know what the yell is until you start and then maybe they will not want to join in. If you use a different click-off for each cheer, they will learn to associate it with the yell. Then when they hear the starting signal, they will know which yell is coming and will start with the first word, even though they missed the announcement.

If your school has never used starting signals, introduce

them slowly. Pick a good one at first and use it with every yell. After the students become familiar with starting signals and learn to watch for them, you can switch to a different click-off for each yell.

HOW TO CONTROL THE VOLUME

You can make your cheers more interesting and effective if you vary the volume. An example of this is a cheer that starts softly and becomes louder with each line. Then it stops at the loudest point, leaving a feeling of drive and tension.

The size and type of motions you use will help determine the volume of the yell. Easy, gentle motions will result in a low volume. Large, vigorous motions will produce louder cheering.

To build up volume on a single word, start back from your cheering section and run at it. The students will yell louder as you approach. To make a word sound louder, surround it with silence. Put a pause before and after the word and it will contrast with the silence. Also, it will give the students a chance to take a deep breath. Here is an example:

Yea, Red! *(silence)* Yea, White! *(silence)*
Yea, Lincoln! *(silence)*
Fight!

In complicated yells, you can control the volume by telling the students what you want, as in this example:

Cheerleaders:	What Do We Want?
Students:	Score!
Cheerleaders:	Louder!
Students:	SCORE!

HOW TO CONTROL THE TEMPO

How fast should your cheer go? It should be fast enough to be peppy but if it is too fast, the words will run together. Every word of your cheer should be clearly understood.

Your yells will be more interesting if they have a variety of speeds. Use short, easily understood words in fast yells and try them at a rally before using them at a game. Slow down yells that have long or complicated words in them.

You can control the silent pauses between words of a cheer with clapping: "Let's Go, Big Team (CLAP-CLAP), Let's Go!"

If you have difficulty establishing the rhythm of a cheer at its beginning, use rhythmical sound effects, such as clapping or drum beats. This is especially good for cheers with unusual rhythms.

HOW TO END A YELL TOGETHER

Your cheers should end the same way they start—sharp and together. This means all cheerleaders must end at the same time.

Give the final motions of every cheer extra practice. When you end with a jump, pose briefly after it. Thank your cheering section for their effort with applause. Develop a definite rhythm to your endings: jump together, pose together, applaud together.

Do not clutter up the end of the yell with random jumping and shouting. Save this for after the yell.

Cheerleaders should have drill-team precision whenever they are on the field. They enter together and go quickly to their positions. The captain announces the yell, all give the starting signal and then lead the cheer. They finish together, applaud their students, and leave together. An organized cheerleading squad encourages organized cheering.

Pace yourself during the game so that you are clean, fresh, and peppy at the end. No matter how tired you are, appear as if you could do the whole game over again. Your cheering section will feel organized and confident if you, they, and the team are still going strong at the end of the game.

An organized, confident cheering section does the best job of supporting its team.

II

Your Main Jobs at the Games

Selecting Cheers

Developing a Balanced Repertoire

REPERTOIRE: All the yells and songs that you and your cheering section have learned.

Have you ever:

1. Called for more touchdowns or baskets when your team was far ahead?

2. Cheered while either team was huddling or calling signals?

3. Led a victory cheer when you were losing?

4. Led a cheer asking for a score when the other team had the ball?

These are mistakes that can be embarrassing to your team, to your school, and to yourself. There are times to cheer and times to keep quiet. When it is time for a cheer, you must choose one that is right for that situation. Not just any yell will do.

Good cheerleaders teach their students a variety of yells so that they will be ready for any situation. If you have just a few cheers that are used over and over, you will wear them out. But you can keep your cheering section alive and enthused with a variety of yells to which you are constantly adding new ones. If the students become bored with a yell, drop it or give it a vacation. With a large, balanced repertoire, you will not even miss it.

Use the following as a guide to classify your yells by *purpose* and *type* to determine if your selection of cheers is varied and balanced.

YELLS BY PURPOSE

I. Special Purpose Yells

A. The Hello Yell. Hello yells have become traditional at most schools and they are usually regarded as a common courtesy. The usual practice is for the home team to welcome the visitor who then replies with a hello yell.

Since you are going to be home team at some games and visitor at others, you either need a hello yell that is worded to meet both occasions or else you need two separate yells. Here is a sample hello yell that is easily changed to meet the occasion:

AS HOME TEAM	AS VISITOR
Hello, Bulldogs,	Hello, Bulldogs,
We've Heard of Your Fame.	We've Heard of Your Fame.
You're in Wildcat Land	We're from Wildcat Land,
But We're Glad You Came!	Let's Have a Big Game!

The hello yell is given before the game starts, so you are not limited on time. It can be a long, novelty-type yell involving cheerleaders, song leaders, and band, or it may be short, strong, and active, designed to get your cheering section warmed up for later yells. Some schools have their cheerleaders lead the hello yell while facing the opponent's rooters. This can be effective, but at least one cheerleader should be left on your side to direct the yell.

B. Yells for Individuals. Most cheering is done at football and basketball games. Since these are team sports, outstanding plays will usually be the result of team effort rather than the effort of just one player. Therefore, your cheering should be done on a team basis. If you give a cheer for a player who has just run 80 yards for a touchdown, you overlook the lineman who made the key block. There are only a few occasions when you should lead cheers for individuals: when the starting lineup is introduced; when individual players leave the game for a rest, and when a player is injured or leaves the game on fouls. At other times, save the individual cheers for individual-type sports, such as boxing or wrestling.

1. Introducing the Starting Lineup.

The public-address announcer will usually introduce the players of both teams by name, number, and position. Normally, he will introduce the visiting team and their coach first and then the home team. There are many ways to cheer for each player on your team as he is introduced. Here are some examples:

ANNOUNCER	CHEERING SECTION
Number 86, Bill Clark	1) Clark!
	2) Bill Clark!
	3) Clark, Bill!
	4) Bill!
	5) Eighty-Six!
	6) Rah!
	7) Bill Clark, Rah!
	8) Clark, Rah!

If your opponents reply to your introductions with a "Who's He?" train your cheering section to respond with "You'll See!" Cheer for your coach when he is introduced. You may cheer for him by name or with a special "coach" cheer.

End your introductions with a cheer for the team so that no one is left out. Do not refer to the nonstarters as "reserves" or "second-string." This tends to downgrade their importance. Each man who is suited-up considers himself a part of the team. Cheer for the "team" and all of your players will feel that you are cheering for them.

When you are the visiting team, use a short "team" yell after your introductions. The announcer will not wait very long before he will start introducing the home team.

2. Individual Players Leaving the Game.

As the game progresses, the coach may rest some of the players by replacing them for a short time. If they have played well, it is customary to give an individual cheer for them. You are cheering for their total efforts, not just for what they did on a single play. When your team is winning by a wide margin, the coach will probably remove the starters to give the reserves experience. If he takes out one or two players at a time, you can cheer for each one. But if he removes them all at once, you will only have time to cheer for the unit as "team."

Some players may be strictly defensive or offensive specialists who enter and leave the game every time the ball changes hands. These do not require individual cheers since they are merely fulfilling their assignments.

3. Cheering for an Injured Player (either team).

While this is to be encouraged, it must be done carefully. It might appear to others that you are pleased to see an opponent injured. You can avoid this misunderstanding if you delay your cheer until the player is either helped from the field or indicates he will remain in the game. Then cheer for him by name or number.

"A Round of Applause and Fifteen Rahs" is a good cheer for this situation. This also applies to the player who fouls out of a basketball game, whether he is on your team or the opponent's. When you give a cheer that is meant as a sincere tribute to an opponent forced to leave the game because of fouls or injuries, you earn the respect and admiration of the students from his school. They will always remember your students as good sports, and this should be just as important as winning the game.

C. Entertainment Yells. Novelty yells are used to entertain the students before the game and at halftime. They fill time and keep the spectators interested while nothing is happening on the field or floor. They include novelty-dance routines by song leaders, special yells to show off gymnastic ability of cheerleaders, or long yells in which the band participates (including novelty songs with school-spirit type words to the tune of a popular song). Most novelty yells will be an instant success with the students, but they can lose their appeal in a hurry if done too often.

II. School-Spirit Yells

Nearly every student thinks his school is "the best." Give him a chance to shout it with an occasional school-spirit yell. These are yells that show that the students are proud of their school and team. The school name, mascot, or colors are usually included in the cheer. Here are the common types of school-spirit yells:

1. Yells that spell out the mascot or school name.

2. Yells that praise your school, mascot, team, or cheering section.

3. Most school-color yells.

School-spirit yells are best when fight yells are not appropriate, such as when you are winning easily, or losing. When you have a big lead, use school-spirit yells that praise your school instead of calling on your team for more points. Be content with victory rather than a score that humiliates your opponent.

If you are losing by a wide margin, your cheering section may lose enthusiasm. Switch to school-spirit yells and let them show that they are still proud of their school even if they are behind.

III. Fight Yells

Fight yells are the cheerleaders' best friend and can be used often. They are short, simple, and LOUD! They are designed to stimulate the students as well as the team. Fight yells are popular with everyone, especially with boys and adults. They are easy to make up and can be used nearly any time during a close game. A cheer that encourages your team to do better is a fight yell, even if it does not have the word "fight" in it. Plan lots of fight yells for your repertoire.

A. Short Fight Yells. Your short fight yells may be from one to five lines. Often, they are four lines long and the final words of the second and fourth lines rhyme. Some of the most effective short yells are just one phrase, such as, "Make that Point!"

Short yells have many advantages. They can be changed easily, they can be squeezed into a short break between plays, and they will keep the students yelling in an organized manner without overworking them. Most students prefer to yell many times for short periods than for one long period. Since short yells are easily learned, the adults will also learn them and join in the cheering.

B. One-Word Yells. Use one-word yells when the time you have is very short, such as when your team breaks the huddle or just before a jump ball. The yell can be any strong word that is appropriate: "GO!" "FIGHT!" "WIN!" "SCORE!" "CHARGE!" Give your cheering section plenty of warning on the yell and use a small preparatory motion before the main motion. This will tell them exactly when to yell. Make the main motion big, simple, and sharp.

C. Chants. Chants are short, one-line yells that are repeated over and over. Each is for a specific purpose, such as, "Hold that Line!" "Make that Point!" "We Want a Touchdown!"

Chants are best when time and space are limited. Another advantage is that they can be stopped at any time. This means you can use them when you want to cheer up to the last possible moment or when you are not sure how much time you have for a cheer.

You can plan your chants ahead of time or make them up as the situation requires. When making up chants, make them a definite rhythm so that they are easy to follow and give the students time to breathe between lines. Since a chant is a form of yell, it should have a beginning and ending.

You have probably heard many chants start softly, gradually build up, and then slowly fade away. These were probably started by a small group of rooters who became tired of waiting for their cheerleaders to think of something. These chants end when the students get tired, which means they will die a slow death rather than end sharply.

Your chants will be far more effective if they are organized. When the occasion calls for a chant, announce it, give a starting signal, lead the chant, and then stop it. Use the same starting and ending signals for your chants, and keep the motions in the chant simple and repetitive. The cheerleaders should always lead the chants in order to control the pace. If the chant is turned over to the students, it will go faster and faster until it is one big mess.

The cheerleader captain decides when the chant is to be stopped. He can do this by giving signals to the other cheerleaders or directly to the cheering section. If he signals just the other cheerleaders, they will need a different motion to indicate that this is the final time through. The captain can signal the cheering section directly by raising both arms over his head indicating two more times. The other cheerleaders continue with the normal motions. The captain drops one arm indicating one more time and then joins the other cheerleaders in giving the cutoff motion.

Your chants will be louder and more effective when you make them a definite length instead of letting them go until the students yell themselves out. Football chants can be repeated five or six times, but two or three times is enough for basketball chants.

YELLS BY TYPE

Here are some of the various types of yells you should have. All the yells in your repertoire need not fit one of these types, but you should have one yell of each type in your repertoire.

I. Student-Action Yells

These yells give the students a chance to participate physically in the yell and gives them a feeling of participating physically in the game. Here is one example: on the final word of a yell, like "Fight!" everyone stands up and throws his fist in the air. Other ways in which the students can participate is through foot stamping, clapping, swaying, etc.

There are certain dangers to student-action yells that you should be aware of: if used too often, the students will get tired of them, and they must be given at the right psychological moment when the students feel a strong desire to do something active. Student-action yells involving spellouts or class yells are good for pregame use as they will show where your nonparticipants are so that you can direct your efforts to including them.

II. *Conversation Yells*

In conversation yells, the cheerleaders ask the students a question and the students give the answer. Sample questions might be, "Who Are We For?" and "Who's Got the Best Team?" Naturally, the students shout back the name of your school. If the answer is always the same, you can change your questions to fit the situation. These are fun yells and can be made up as you go along. But be sure the students know how they are supposed to answer.

If you have a microphone or megaphone, the cheerleader captain can use it to ask the questions while the other cheerleaders lead the answers. Use just one motion for the answer and do not change it. When the motion is consistent, the students will recognize it and will not be confused when you change the question.

III. *Echo Yells*

On an echo yell, the students repeat exactly what the cheerleaders say. The echo yell is best for a long yell since the only ones who must memorize it are the cheerleaders. One of the cheerleaders is delegated to lead the cheering section while the others give the first part of the yell. The words should be simple and the phrase short. Otherwise, the yell can become a jumbled mess. Here is a sample opening to an echo yell:

Cheerleaders:	Now We've Got a Team,
Students:	NOW WE'VE GOT A TEAM,
Cheerleaders:	That's Really Neat!
Students:	THAT'S REALLY NEAT!

IV. *Sound-Effect Yells*

Sound-effect yells involve weird or unusual sounds with no particular meaning. Although they are part of a yell, they are generally used for a humorous effect. Therefore, they should be used only once or twice a game and only when the students are in the proper mood. Sound-effect yells may use a bell, horn, or just sounds from the students, such as whistling, animal or train sounds, accompanied by appropriate poses by the cheerleaders.

V. Spellouts

Spellouts are good general yells to include in your repertoire, and there are several ways of leading them:

1. The students say the letter with the cheerleaders.

2. The cheerleaders say the letter and then lead the students in repeating it.

3. The cheerleader captain asks for a letter and the other cheerleaders lead the students. Here is an example:

Captain:	Give me an A!
Students:	A!
Captain:	Now a B!
Students:	B!
Captain:	Try a C!
Students:	C!

All of these types of spellouts force pauses between each letter so that it sounds better than if the letters run together. Another way to improve spellouts is to make them gradually faster and louder. When you do this, put long pauses between the letters when you start so that you can get brief pauses in between the letters when you speed up. Always finish your spellout by saying the word that was spelled.

When to Cheer and When not to

At every game there will be many opportunities for you to lead cheers. In a matter of seconds, you must be able to recognize the opportunity and choose an appropriate cheer. If you hesitate, the chance will be lost or taken by the opposing cheerleaders.

How can you tell when it is time for a cheer? First, look over these suggestions for times when it is best *not* to cheer:

1. While an injured player is lying on the floor or field. Wait until he gets up and then cheer for him.

2. While a basketball player is shooting foul shots. This is poor sportsmanship.

3. While your band is playing or about to play. Work out a system with your band director for signaling when there is to be a cheer and when there is to be a song. A good band- and song-leading squad is an important part of any cheering section. Share the time-outs.

4. While announcements are being made over the public-address system or while someone else is performing. The cheering section can focus its attention on just one thing at a time. Do not try to give a cheer when others have the spotlight.

5. While the ball is in play, since the students will probably watch the game instead of you. But here are a few exceptions:

a) The "sssssssssssss—Boom!" for football kickoffs is widely used.

b) Many schools count down the final 10 seconds of a game (but have a squad member watch the game and stop the countdown if a time-out is taken).

c) Easy chants. The students can usually stay together on these without watching the cheerleaders.

Now, when are good times to cheer? You can use cheers and songs whenever play is stopped and nothing else is happening. For practice, watch some football and basketball games on television and look for cheering opportunities. At all games, there are periods before the game, at halftime, and between quarters.

Then there are time-outs. These are normally taken by a team to stop the clock when time is short, or for a rest period. If a full time-out is taken, you have one minute for a cheer or a song. But if the time-out was taken to merely stop the clock, play may resume in a few seconds. If the water boy goes on the field at a football game, you know that a full time-out will be taken. But be wary of time-outs taken near the end of the half or the end of the game. If you are not sure if you have a full time-out, use short yells or chants that can be stopped at any time.

At basketball games a full time-out will be taken if the whole team goes over to talk to the coach. In football you have a few moments from the time one play ends until the players huddle. Then you have another break when the team leaves the huddle, but before they start calling signals. You can fit short or one-word yells into these periods but you should warn the cheering section ahead of time, e.g., "After the next play, Let's have a 'GO!—FIGHT!—WIN!' " or, "Let's have a 'CHARGE!' when they break the huddle."

Football teams can take a maximum of 25 seconds between plays and the average huddle lasts about 15 seconds. In basketball there are pauses from the time officials call fouls or jumps until play resumes. You can fit cheers into these periods if you are alert. As soon as the referee halts play, announce the yell and complete it before the ball is put into play. When leading a cheer for a player who has left the game, try to finish it before play gets underway again.

Once you know how to spot cheering opportunities, how do you pick the right cheer for that particular occasion? The secret is *plan ahead*. Watch the game closely and follow the action. If your football team is on the move, the next cheer should be one that will encourage them to keep the drive going. This means a fight yell or a "We Want a Touchdown" chant if they are threatening to score.

Decide which cheer you will use and lead it at the first opportunity. Do not waste time trying to choose a yell after play has been stopped. As soon as you finish a cheer, start planning the next one. Relate it to the course of play and try to anticipate the next cheering opportunity. In football you should always have an alternate cheer in mind for a sudden setback, such as a lost fumble or intercepted pass.

Read the local sports pages before each game. Sportswriters can give you tips on what to expect from the opposing team. If they say that your next opponent has a star passer, you can make up special yells or chants, such as, "Put the Pressure on Bill Lester!"

As the game progresses, one of the teams may start pulling ahead. If they gain a sizable lead, you should begin thinking about these suggestions for winning and losing situations.

WHEN WINNING. If victory appears certain, drop the fight yells and chants of the "We Want More" nature and switch to school-spirit cheers that praise your team and school.

WHEN LOSING. If it appears that you will lose the game or if your team is on a losing streak, drop cheers that mention victory or win. Use school-spirit and fight cheers that call on your team to do its best.

The following chart can help you fit the cheer to the situation. An "X" in the square indicates the type or types of cheers that would be appropriate for the listed situation.

Here is one final comment about choosing the right cheer for the right moment. You may pick the perfect cheer to fit the occasion and see it flop because your rooters were not in the mood. Maybe the first half was close and hard fought. There were many time-outs and you led a lot of cheers. The score suddenly became lopsided in the second half, and your fans lost interest in cheering or got tired. Use fewer cheers and try songs instead. (But if they will not sing, do not keep trying.) Give the fans a rest. Perhaps something will happen in the game to get their interest up again and then you can try more yells. But do not try to lead a cheer just because you have an opportunity. If you know the fans are not in the mood, it is better to skip it.

SITUATION	Special Purpose Yells	FIGHT YELLS			Entertainment Yells	Short Songs	School-Spirit Yells
		Short Yells	One-word Yells	Chants			
FOR ALL GAMES							
Pregame	Hello & Introductions				×	×	×
Between quarters						×	×
Halftime					×	×	×
Time-outs—You're ahead						×	×
Time-outs—You're losing		×		×			×
Time-outs—Game in doubt		×	×	×			
Injured players	Individual						
FOOTBALL ONLY							
Between plays			×				
Out of the huddle			×				
Your team about to score		×		×			
After you score						×	
Opponents about to score		×	×	×			
First down, your team			×	×			
First down, opponents				×			
BASKETBALL ONLY							
Player fouls out	Individual						
Before foul shot			×				
Before jump ball			×				
After your basket			×				
Opponents stall				×			
During foul shot	SILENCE						

5

Crowd Psychology

To get as many people as possible to participate with you in organized cheering, you need to know as much as you can about them. Once you have this information, you can decide which actions on your part will get the best response from them.

People who attend games like to get into the act. By participating in the cheering section, they feel that they are taking an active part in the game. Your job is to help them do it in an organized way.

Spectators are made up of all kinds of people, with all kinds of likes and dislikes. Boys like yells with two or three powerful-sounding words accompanied by simple motions. They usually like student-participation cheers where they can throw their fist and make funny noises. Girls will participate in nearly any type of yell but like the "cute" ones best. Adults generally prefer simple yells that they can learn quickly and not feel ridiculous saying. If the yell sounds childish to them, they probably will not participate.

Obviously, it is hard to please everyone all the time. But you should try to make your yells appeal to as many people as possible. Do this by building a balanced and varied repertoire of cheers. Learn to sense the mood of the spectators and observe their reaction to each yell.

If they are not cheering with you, do not criticize them. After all, they came to watch the game. Maybe you need to improve your yells or perhaps you are asking for the wrong yell for particular situations. You may have asked for too many yells, and they are tired. When the game is exciting, they will yell on their own and will be hard to organize.

If you are not getting the response you want, review the situation. Did you ask for the right cheer at the right time? If your choices were good, assume that the spectators were not inspired, so you will have to fire them up.

Get their interest with a short yell that has been popular in the past. Sometimes an amusing chant that teases your opponent will do the trick; or often competitions between boys and girls will stimulate interest. Avoid direct competitions between the students and adults. In these cases the adults usually lose and then they will ignore you the rest of the game. If you have a competition, give the loser a second chance if time permits.

Make your competitions positive. Do not ask, "Are You With Us, Juniors?" Instead, try a "Now Let's Have One Big FIGHT! from the Juniors." Never ask a question that can be answered wrong deliberately.

One of the best ways to develop enthusiasm is to be enthusiastic and peppy yourself. Sooner or later it will spread to the spectators. Do not let the ho-hum attitude of a group of students affect you. *Keep smiling* regardless of what happens!

Sometimes the students will do poorly on a cheer because they did not hear it announced. Announce each yell loudly and clearly several times if possible. Do not try to announce a cheer while people are yelling. Wait until they quiet down.

Often the attention of the spectators will be on the game when you try to announce your yell. Waving or signaling will get the attention of only a few. You are going to have to SHOUT! Use a microphone or megaphone. When using a megaphone, do not wave it the length of the spectators while announcing the cheer. Point it at one section, announce the yell, and then point it at another section and repeat the announcement.

If several cheerleaders have megaphones, each tells his own

section what the cheer will be. If you want to squeeze a short yell in between plays, warn the students ahead of time. Say, "Let's have a 'Go-Team-Go!' when they come out of the huddle."

HOW TO MAKE THE STUDENTS FEEL THAT THEY ARE A PART OF THE GAME

The important point here is to explain to the students at the rally why you are going to ask them to do certain things. For example, explain that you are going to ask them to be quiet when the team is huddling near your sideline and that you are going to ask for especially loud yells when your team needs a lift. Let the students know you plan to lead them in a manner that will make them an active part of the game. When the game is over, they can take pride in knowing that they did their part well whether the team won or lost.

GETTING ALONG WITH THE STUDENTS

Thank the students with applause after each cheer or song. Look directly at them and clap toward them to show that you really mean it. Compliment them when they do a particularly good job, or at least better than last time. They will try even harder next time.

If something goes wrong with a yell, do not blame or argue with the students. Analyze what went wrong and try to correct it. Practice the cheer at the next pep rally before using it again during a game.

If things are not going right, do not make speeches. Your job is to lead cheers, not to lecture. Maintain your dignity at all times. When you are tempted to demonstrate your disgust for something, remember that your school considers you as someone special. As their leader would they want you to act that way?

Adults can be a big help in making your cheers sound good. If you act in a mature manner, you will have their respect. You can do this and keep the respect of the teen-agers too. Students expect their leaders to show mature judgment.

Crowd control is also your job. Do not let someone else

take over. The students will stay with you if you give them something they can follow.

Learn to "feel" when the students have an urge to yell. Lead them in a cheer when they are in the right mood for one. If they ask for a specific yell and it is appropriate, lead it. This will help your popularity and build your reputation for ability to control a crowd.

Something is wrong when the students start their own cheers or chants. You may not be leading enough cheers or you may not be choosing the right times to cheer. If their cheers are in poor taste, ignore them or drown them out with a regular yell. Do not let the students run the show.

Be sensitive to the mood of the students all through the game and especially near the end. If they are restless and want to yell, keep them busy. If they are tired or prefer to just watch the game, give them a rest.

The students will often reflect the manner in which the cheerleaders behave. If you display discourtesy, lack of interest, or a bad temper, they will tend to show these feelings. When they do they become difficult to control. Look organized yourself. A squad that cannot make up its mind or stay together discourages the students and dampens their enthusiasm for cheering.

An organized cheering section can support its team better than a disorganized one. One of your goals should be to finish each game as organized as you began. When you do you keep the enthusiasm of the students up for the entire game, and your team gets the full support it deserves.

CROWD CONTROL PROBLEMS AND HOW YOU
APPROACH THEM
How to Stop Booing

Booing must be stopped instantly or it will spread like wildfire. It is usually started by just a few people and then picked up by others. Stay alert and you can anticipate situations that may draw boos from your cheering section, such as a crucial or unpopular penalty. There are two ways to stop booing if you act quickly: drown out the boos with your loudest yell or chant, or divert the attention of those doing the booing with a chant or student-action yell.

What to Do with Clusters of Uncooperative Students

A club or group of students may get together and start their own cheers. They are looking for attention, and if you give it to them you can make them work for you. Charm them into joining you. Recognize them, identify them, and enlist their aid. But do it without embarrassing them. Here is an example: "We're real glad to see the Hot Rod Club out in full force tonight and we'd like to have them help us with the sound effects on the WHOOP! yell. O.K.? Bill over there will cue you. Now, let's have the WHOOP! yell and let's really hear it when we get to your part, Hot Rodders."

How to Contend with Individual Hecklers and Wise Guys

These may be students or adults. In either case ignore them. They are seeking attention and if they get it, they will be joined by others. Do not argue or talk to them. Just smile and continue with what you are doing. If you are not bothered by them, they will get discouraged and quit. Every paying customer has a right to act like a nut if he wants to.

What to Do if the Students Are Tired or Unresponsive

Let them rest. When they are not yelling well, you will have a natural tendency to try all the harder. The more you try, the worse results you will get. Drop organized cheering for a while. When something exciting happens in the game, they may become interested and want to yell again.

What to Do with Air Horns and Sound-Effect Devices

Ask your school authorities to ban them. The kids who bring them usually are the uncooperative types who want to attract attention to themselves. They will blow them at the wrong time and spoil your cheers. If you need special sound effects, ask the band to provide them. They will cooperate and provide them only on cue.

How to Get People to Stay to the End of the Game

Give them a reason to stay. Have a traditional countdown of the final 10 seconds of the game. Sing the alma mater, announce a Player of the Game, or give an award to someone. Ask your coach or team captain to speak to the cheering section briefly after each game. Make the end of the game special, and the fans will stay.

In some leagues it has become traditional for all players, coaches, cheerleaders, and song leaders to remain on the field after the game while each school sings its alma mater. All players take off their helmets during the singing and stand in front of the school that is doing the singing. The losing side is first, followed by the winning side. If you can get players and coaches to stay on the field a few moments after the game, you will get the fans to stay.

If a few students start to leave early, it is important to catch the first one and this should be done at the first game of the season. If you can stop the first one, you can probably keep the rest. Single him out by name if necessary. Say, "Hey, Smith, what's your hurry?" If you embarrass him, it probably will not happen again and others will take the hint. But if you let some get away, you will not be able to hold the others. The first one is the crucial one.

III

Your Main Jobs at School

6

Successful Pep Rallies

How to Plan and Conduct Them

A successful pep rally is well planned, adequately rehearsed, and smoothly conducted. It builds school spirit in the team and the student body. In many schools, responsibility for planning and encouraging rallies rests with the cheerleaders and pep clubs. If planning rallies is new for you or if you feel that your rallies need improving, this chapter will help you.

HOW OFTEN SHOULD YOU HAVE RALLIES?
Once a week during the athletic season. You will want your rallies to be popular with the students, and if you schedule too many, the students will become bored with them. Plan a rally for each football game and one for every other basketball game. If you have an important midweek game, you can supplement the regular rally with a short lunch-period rally on the day of the game. Watch for opportunities for special rallies, such as a team send-off or a welcome-home rally for your team following an important away game. You should try to have at least one cheerleader at any place where students are likely to gather to express support for your team. Cheerleaders can make a definite contribution at frosh, interclass games, or informal rallies.

WHERE SHOULD YOU HOLD THE RALLY?

If you have the support of the school authorities, you should be able to use the gym or auditorium. It is best to have facilities large enough for the whole student body to meet together. If the facilities are too small, you will have to hold your rally in shifts, with separate rallies for juniors, seniors, etc.

Another possibility is holding your rally prior to the game. Then you can have it in the stands or nearby. If the rally is not held in the stands, you can march or serpentine to the game after the rally.

WHEN IS THE BEST TIME FOR A RALLY?

This depends on your school. Some schools excuse the last class 15 to 20 minutes early on game day. Others hold their rallies during the lunch period. Some prefer to have the rally after school or before the game. Work out the plan that is best for your school in cooperation with your principal.

Most cheerleaders feel that the ideal time is at the close of school on game day. This gives them a chance to build enthusiasm and interest so that more students will attend the game. If the game is on a Saturday, hold your rally before the game and use other methods to get the students to attend.

HOW LONG SHOULD THE RALLY LAST?

Make it as short as possible and keep the individual segments short. The students will get bored quickly, especially if asked to do too much yelling and singing. Start your rally on time, move quickly through it without any delays and then end it on time. A short but peppy rally will send the students off in high spirits, hardly able to wait for game time. But if you overwork them at the rally, they will not have the enthusiasm they need for the game. Fifteen to twenty minutes is about the right length for a well-planned rally.

WHAT SHOULD BE INCLUDED IN THE RALLY?

Anything that will build school spirit, raise enthusiasm and interest in the game and your team. Include school fight songs, traditional yells, gags, and stunts, and talks by players, coaches, faculty members, or student officers.

Introduce new yells at the rallies. You should teach one new yell at each rally and two at the beginning of the season (but never more than two at one rally). If the students know that a new yell will be taught, they will have one more reason for attending since they will not want to be left out when the new yell is used at the game. Besides the new yell, you can teach chants, slogans, and short songs since these are easy to remember and can be learned quickly.

Introduce the players and coaches at the rallies. This should be emphasized early in the season so that the students will recognize the players in the halls. Even after the players are well known, the students like to see and applaud their favorites. Think up novel ways to introduce the team or some of the players at each rally. Here are some examples to start with:

1. Entrance through an archway.

2. Escorted by school beauty queens.

3. Unusual dress, such as "football through the ages" or "basketball as it might be played in other countries."

Always check your ideas out with the coach. He may have some suggestions for you as well as be able to encourage co-operation from the team.

How about the alma mater? Usually not. Most school alma maters are hymnlike and, while inspirational, do not encourage enthusiasm or loud singing. Save the alma mater for the end of the game and use peppy fight songs at the rally.

HOW DO YOU PLAN RALLIES?

The best way is with a planning committee. If you do not have one, ask your school president to help you organize one. The committee can meet at lunch period or after school and work out the plans and details for the rallies. Here are some of the people that should be on the committee:

1. All cheerleaders and song leaders.

2. Representatives from the band, pep club, and service clubs.

3. A team member or manager.

4. At least one member of the student council.

Ask your principal to name a faculty member to advise and counsel. This should be a faculty member who will encourage the students to do the planning and not try to take over the committee.

You should also try to have a couple of students who can do art work and make posters and signs. And put your master of ceremonies on the committee. This should be a boy who is good on a microphone and who will M.C. all of your rallies. When he is in on the initial planning, it is easy for him to prepare his script to keep the rally running smoothly.

Do not worry about making your committee too large. The more you have on it, the more ideas you will get and the more ways you can divide the work. And a large number of committee members will be helpful when it comes to getting props for skits and stunts.

Usually, the cheerleader captain or pep-club president is the permanent chairman of the committee but he appoints a different chairman for each rally. This encourages the rally chairmen to work extra hard on their own rallies as well as helping as much as they can on the other rallies. The permanent chairman decides when and where the committee is to meet. This should be on a regular schedule. If the rallies are on Fridays, plan the first meeting for the previous Monday. If you do not get the rally planned on Monday, you still have four days to work on it. But meet every day until the rally is set.

Once the details are worked out, have an outline of the rally duplicated and given to everyone who will participate. See that the coach, band director, and any special guests are fully aware of their role in the rally.

The easiest and quickest way to plan successful pep rallies is to develop a format that can be followed for each rally. Here is a sample:

ORDER	ACTIVITY	PARTICIPANTS
1.	Class Yells	Students
2.	Pledge of Allegiance	Student Body President
3.	Yell	Cheerleaders
4.	Stunt	Pep Club
5.	Victory Song	Band and Song Leaders
6.	New Yell	Cheerleaders
7.	Talk	Coach or Player
8.	Gag	Bill G. & George T.
9.	Traditional Yell	Cheerleaders
10.	Fight Song	Band and Song Leaders

Once you have a format you can make changes, additions, and deletions for each rally, but at least you have a starting point. Notice how easy it is to designate the duties with a format: the cheerleaders plan the yells; the band representatives and song leaders decide on the songs; the team representative lines up a speaker, etc.

HOW DO YOU GET THE STUDENTS TO COME TO THE RALLIES?

Give them a good reason for coming and develop a reputation for putting on good rallies. If your rally is held during class time, you will have no problem. The students either go to the rally or they go to study hall. They *do not* go home! (Your principal will be glad to enforce this for you.)

If your rally is held after school or during the lunch period, you may have to think up some gimmicks to get the students to attend. If you have a successful team and a lot of student enthusiasm, your job is that much easier. Most students will attend voluntarily or allow themselves to be dragged along. But suppose your team is not doing well. This is when your school and team needs the extra enthusiasm and interest that can be generated by a pep rally. Here are a few ideas to attract students to your rallies:

Ugly Man Contest. Select a number of handsome and popular boys in your school who will go along with the gag (include players if you can). On the day of the rally have them dress up in old, ragged, and torn clothing and have your drama coach make them up for scars, black eyes, and missing teeth. The object is to make each boy as ugly as possible. At the rally the students vote by applause for the winner, who is given an award or recognition.

Grub Day. All students are asked to wear old or mismatched clothes on the day of the rally. They wear two different kinds of shoes and socks, a sweater or jacket on backward or inside-out, or they may have their hair combed in an unusual manner or not at all. At the rally, choose the "grubbiest" boy and girl for awards.

How about student talent acts? You probably have many students in your school with a variety of talents. Some are pretty good but others may still be just learning or have uninteresting talents. If you use student talent, you are usually forced to give everyone a chance or you will have some unhappy students and angry parents. Play it safe and save your student talent for the talent show.

Faculty talent is different and you should use it if you have a talented faculty member. School majorettes can give twirling performances while the band plays since twirling is part of their job as majorette.

Whenever you consider anything for a rally, ask yourself, "Will it be peppy and enthusiastic?" If not, politely turn it down.

HOW MANY YELLS SHOULD YOU GIVE AT A RALLY?

Do a couple of traditional ones and teach a new one. Students would rather learn the yells in the privacy of the rally than at the game where they are surrounded by the general public and students from another school. Think of the rally as the rehearsal for your rooting section and the game as the performance.

HOW TO TEACH A NEW YELL

First, the yells should be simple and easy to learn. The

students should be able to memorize them quickly so that they do not have to look at slips of paper at the game (if they remember to bring them). Have your new yell printed in the school paper before the rally or have it mimeographed and passed out ahead of time as an advertisement for the rally. This gives the kids a chance to become familiar with the words before you start teaching the yell. Here is a good method for teaching a new yell:

1. *The cheerleaders demonstrate the yell by going through the words and motions at normal speed.*

2. *The captain says the words over the microphone while the other cheerleaders demonstrate the motions.*

3. *The motions are done slowly while the captain says the words over the microphone and the students join in.*

4. *This is repeated, but a little faster.*

5. *The captain rejoins the other cheerleaders, and the yell is done with the students at normal speed.*

If they have not learned it at this point, the yell is too complicated. *What about class yells?* Class yells ("Yea, Seniors," etc.), are an excellent way to get the rally started. They warm up the students for yelling later in the program and give your rally a *BIG NOISE* start.

One way to get a rally moving in a hurry is to ask your band director to make up a small pep band. These students meet somewhere in the halls with their instruments just before the rally is scheduled to begin. They start playing a fight song and march through the halls. As they pass each classroom, the students are dismissed and fall in behind the band, cheerleaders, and song leaders. By the time the band has reached the rally area, it has picked up the whole student body. The students then give their class yells until the student body president signals for quiet and leads the school in the Pledge of Allegiance. This will give the rest of the band time to get their instruments and join the pep band. Here are some other ways to build interest in your rallies:

1. Advertise throughout the week with posters, signs, bulletins, and notices in your school paper.

2. At the game, honor the player or players who were outstanding at your last game.

3. Ask one of the coaches to speak briefly about your next opponent.

HOW ABOUT THE HOMECOMING RALLY?

Make this a special rally that the alums can take part in. Try to schedule it for a time and place so that they can attend. Have alumni speakers, cheerleaders, maybe even an alumni band. Your yells and songs should be traditional ones that the alumni would know. Some schools include the singing of "Auld Lang Syne" as it is an appropriate song that everyone knows.

Sometimes the cheerleaders are asked to handle all the homecoming arrangements. If this responsibility falls on you, here are some important areas you should consider:

1. An alumni chairman and alumni dance committee.
2. Queen competition.
3. Publicity and promotion.
4. Decorations and displays.
5. Awards.
6. Dance committee for students.

SHOULD YOU PLAN A BONFIRE RALLY?

By all means. They require a lot of thought and preparation but they are fun for the students and townspeople. The best idea is to schedule just one a season and use it for a special game, such as the homecoming game. When you have just one bonfire rally, the students look forward to it and participate far more than they would if you had several.

After clearing your idea with school authorities, check with your local Fire Department. They can help you choose a site, get a fire permit if needed, and offer suggestions. They will probably want to be nearby during the rally, just in case. If you talk to them ahead of time, they will be willing to cooperate. However, they can put a quick end to future bonfire rallies if you do not notify them. Next, check with your local Police Department. They can be helpful in blocking off streets and keeping traffic out of the way.

Once you have decided on a time and place, you will need wood for the fire. Sometimes this can be done by a committee who collects the wood and piles it up before the rally. However, many a bonfire rally has gone up in smoke early when the opposing school heard about an unguarded woodpile.

An easier and safer way to collect wood is to have a class (usually the Freshman), bring the wood to the rally. If your school is small, you can have a contest to see which class brings the most wood.

Once you get the fire going, plan on school songs, yells, stunts, and speakers, just as you would for a regular rally. If you have a majorette who can twirl a fire baton, this is the perfect spot for her number. Throw a dummy dressed as your opponent on the fire. Afterward, you can have a street dance if weather permits or a serpentine through the streets.

The bonfire rally should be held in the evening the day before the game. Get out a lot of publicity, such as posters in the stores and articles in the local newspaper to encourage the public to attend. Ask your coach to introduce the team at the rally as this may be the only chance for some of the townspeople to see the players without their uniforms and helmets on. After the rally is over, have someone delegated to see that the area is cleaned up to the satisfaction of the Fire Department.

WHAT IF YOUR TEAM IS ON A LOSING STREAK?

Make "Do Your Best, Win or Lose" your rally theme. Take the approach that your team will try hard and give its best effort and that the students should do the same. Emphasize the idea that there is honor in fighting hard, whether you win or lose.

Ask one of the coaches or a representative of the players to give a talk explaining some of the reasons the team has been losing (critical penalties, injuries, etc.). Games are often lost due to factors beyond the control of your team. The students will not mind losses so much if they have some understanding as to the cause.

Pep up your rallies with lots of funny gags. When referring to your team after they have lost, take the attitude of "That's O.K. You're still our boys and we're proud of you." Show the team that you are still behind them and they will try even harder to win the next game.

THE MAIN PURPOSE OF A PEP RALLY IS TO BOOST SCHOOL SPIRIT!

Memorize that sentence and think of it whenever you plan a rally. If an idea does not meet this requirement, change it or reject it. There are only two kinds of rallies—good ones and flops. Use the following suggestions as a guide and you can avoid putting on flops:

1. Plan a balanced and varied program.

2. Rehearse each portion carefully and see that everyone knows his part.

3. Have a good announcer who will keep the program moving.

4. Cooperate with everyone concerned—the coach, team, band director, principal, etc. They will cooperate with you.

5. Keep your rallies short, simple, and peppy.

7

Ideas for Building School Spirit

Building school spirit is one of your year-around jobs as a cheerleader. But just what is school spirit? Actually, it is easier to describe than to define. If your school has good school spirit, the students are proud of their school, their teachers, and their classmates. They participate in as many school activities as possible and are enthusiastic supporters of the team. They brag about their school, their team, and the accomplishments of their classmates. They think of their school as an exclusive club and they are proud to be members.

But if the students have a "ho-hum" attitude toward school activities and attend games only when they are in the mood, you have a school-spirit problem. There are many simple things you can do to improve school spirit. As you read the following suggestions, you will probably come up with some ideas of your own.

INCREASING STUDENT IDENTIFICATION

One of the first steps toward improving school spirit is to develop a feeling of togetherness among your students. Give them ways to identify with their school, such as hats, badges, streamers, or small megaphones. Tell them to dress alike for the games by wearing their school sweaters, jackets, or white shirts and blouses. Reserve the choicest seats in the cheering section for those who go along with the plan and you will have no trouble getting cooperation.

Another popular device is the use of bumper stickers or decals for the students to put on their cars. These can have your school name or a slogan, e.g., "Pass Carefully—Wildcat at Wheel!" Most of these items can be ordered through a school supply store and sold to the students at cost, or used as a fund-raising method by the cheerleaders.

Do not forget the team. Decorate their locker room before the game, and if they are going on a bus put lots of signs on it.

BUILDING UP INTEREST IN THE GAMES

Show off your school spirit at the games. Get as many students to attend as possible, organize them into a cheering section, and let them cheer your team to victory.

It is not hard but it may take a little work and thought. First, how do you get the kids to go to the games? If your team is good, your work is done. The students will flock to the games to watch them win. But if you are having an off-year and losing regularly, you are going to have to work up interest among the students to go to the games.

Posters and cartoons in the halls will serve as constant reminders. Change the posters each week so that they relate to your next opponent. The simplest idea is to show your mascot doing something to your opponent's mascot.

Think up a slogan for each game, such as "Fill the Air with Bear Hair!" Use this slogan in your posters. Make up badges or cutouts of your mascot with the slogan printed on them and have the students wear them to school and to the game. Tell the students to greet each team member they meet during the week with the slogan instead of the usual hello. Use the slogan as a chant at the rally and at the game. Your slogan becomes the "theme" for the game.

If you have trouble coming up with catchy slogans, ask the students for suggestions. Have a contest with prizes for those who submit the best slogans.

Girls sometimes complain that they do not understand the

games so they do not attend. Have a class for them. If you cannot use school time, have the class during the lunch period. Ask one of the coaches to serve as instructor. They will be pleased to do it because they know it will mean more support for the team. *Caution:* Keep the boys out! They will only try to embarrass the girls with their knowledge of the game. If enough boys are genuinely interested in learning about the game, set up a class for them, too.

The students will be more interested in the games if they know the players. In small schools this will not be a problem since most students will know everyone. But at large schools, many students may not recognize the football players out of uniform. Set up displays with pictures of your players. Ask the coach to introduce the team at your first pep rally. See that each player comes on the stage as his name is called so that the students can associate names and faces. Have a special section reserved for the team at the rallies.

Establish a "Player of the Week" award for your team. The coach can pick the winner. Present the award at the next rally or, better yet, immediately after the game. This can be a good way to get the students to stay until the end of the game.

When playing away from home, encourage as many students to go as possible. Publicize the rooters' bus or, if you cannot use buses, help the students organize car pools and rides. The world's greatest cheerleader would look rather silly trying to lead a cheering section of just five people or so. The more students you can get to the games, the more yelling you will get. And the more yelling you get, the better the job you will do as cheerleader.

STUNTS AND GAGS

You can use stunts, skits, and gags to build up interest in the team and the games. They can be used at rallies, lunch periods, or other student assemblies. If you have a particularly good stunt, use it at halftime. Here are three things to think about when using stunts and gags:

1. Be sure they are in good taste; as a cheerleader, you

cannot afford to take a chance on something questionable.

2. Clear them ahead of time with your faculty adviser or principal.

3. If someone is to be the butt of a joke, he *must* be clued in ahead of time and give his consent. If warned ahead of time, most people will go along with a gag. (The rest of the students do not need to know that the "goat" has been clued in.)

If one of the cheerleaders is to be a part of a gag, he should not lose his dignity in the process. The students are supposed to laugh at the joke, not the cheerleader. Here are some ideas and suggestions for gags and stunts:

Symbolic. Stunts symbolic of victory are easy to make up. Throw darts at an image of your opponent, stage a fight between mascots, do parodies on well-known poetry, television shows or commercials, fairy tales, or comic strips. Use a basketball as a crystal ball for a "swami" to see victory. Stage a mock trial for your opponent, operate on him or bury him.

Teasing. Use representations of your opponent as the butt of a joke, such as having several hefty boys dressed up as the opponent's cheerleaders and leading a silly yell. Have your own squad present a yell for your opponent, using a standard cheer but with the strong words changed to delicate ones or given in a high-pitched voice or in a weird or silly accent.

Contests. Pick a "mystery person" at your school. Tell all the students they must find this person by asking one another a question or giving a slogan, like "Beat the Wildcats!" The first person to say the slogan to the mystery person is the winner. Have a contest to guess the identity of players. Give clues that refer to that player's performance in the last game, such as, "He threw the opposing quarterback for a 12-yard loss in the second quarter." This will encourage the students to go to the games so that they will understand the clues. Stage an Ugly Man contest, using some good-looking and willing boys. Have a bathing-suit contest for some of your best-looking girls. Every boy in school will attend! For a prize that will not cost you anything, ask the coach to donate an old football or basketball that is no longer used. Have all the players and coaches autograph it.

Backward and Reverse. Declare a "Backward Day" where everything is done backward and each student wears some article of clothing on backward. At the rally, the players can take the role of majorettes or band members, the teachers lead cheers and the coach or principal acts as janitor and sweeps off the stage.

Pantomimes. You can use these to improve sportsmanship or student behavior at the games. Set up make-believe bleachers and have students act out different types of rooters, such as lovers, gum chewers, squirmers, eaters, the up-and-downer, and Miss Bubble Gum.

Conquering Hero. One of the players or your mascot rescues a cheerleader, song leader, or majorette from the clutches of the nasty opponent mascot.

Game Preview. Stage a mock game, using girls or the smallest boys in school as players. Naturally, your team wins.

Here is a list of topics to think of when trying to create a new skit or stunt:
1. School traditions.
2. Your mascot, nickname, or school colors.
3. Your opponents' mascot.
4. Current events.
5. Historical characters or events.

Sometimes you may want a stunt or gag that is just for laughs and does not relate to the game. Start with these ideas:
1. Teasing a teacher or the principal (if they will go along with it).
2. Pantomime a hit tune.
3. Do a history of cheerleading with appropriate dress and yells for cavemen, Romans, Pilgrims, cowboys, etc.
4. Present a cheerleading-around-the-world with the

cheerleaders dressing and cheering as from another country. Show how football or basketball might be played in another country.

5. Look into the future and picture prominent school personalities as they might be in 20 years.

6. Use guest cheerleaders, such as popular students, principal, players, or cooks.

Since stunts and gags depend mainly on visual effect, give careful consideration to casting, costuming, and props. Beware of the "ham" character who tries to hog the stunt.

This is only a beginning list for building school spirit. Circumstances and situations are different in every school. What works at one school might flop at another. Only *you* will know what is best for your own school and you will probably find that your own ideas are the most popular ones.

How to Think Up Gags. The rally committee will probably think of enough gags to keep the rallies going for a while. When they run out, you can start a "Gag of the Week" contest for the students. When someone suggests a good one, use it and recognize the person who submitted it. Gags should be used only once and never repeated.

How to Get Stunts. Although there are a number of stunt books in libraries, you may find it more fun to make up your own. First, make a list of the words or phrases that have some connection with your school, your mascot, or school colors. For example, Roosevelt High School: Roughriders, Teddies, Bull Moose, "carry a big stick." Now make a similar list for your opponents. Then compare the two lists to see if you can hit on a combination that will lend itself to a stunt. If not, make up a third list. This would contain words and phrases associated with a current event, such as an election, or an approaching holiday such as Halloween or Thanksgiving.

Have someone write the lists on a blackboard where everyone on the committee can see them. Others will suggest additional words and soon you will have some ideas. Write the ideas on the board until one either becomes the stunt or several are combined. You will find this an entertaining way of getting your programs planned, as well as creating unique and original stunts.

Once you have decided on your gags and stunts, designate the persons who are to participate, and determine what props are needed. Appoint students to furnish the props and plan a rehearsal. Now your rally format is complete and you are ready to start tying the segments together. Schedule the events so that they balance the program and you do not have all the yells in one place. Once you have decided on the order, your M.C. can begin work on his script. Have copies of the final program made up so that each participant can have a copy.

For your first rally of the season, you should plan a full rehearsal to establish the pattern. Everyone should walk through his part while the M.C. reads his script. This would get people used to the idea of entering and leaving the stage at the proper time. The speaker and band director should be on hand for this rehearsal so that they can see what their parts will be. It is not necessary to go through the actual yells or songs, but have the cheerleaders and song leaders practice entering and leaving so that they will know their cue.

For future rehearsals, you should have a quick run-through of anything new, and to show someone who has never been in a rally before how and where to enter the stage.

Sportsmanship

How to Make a Good Reputation for Your School

What Is Sportsmanship? It is the ability to accept defeat without complaint; victory without bragging, and to treat your opponents with fairness and courtesy. "It's how you *play* the game that counts—not whether you win or lose." This is the meaning of sportsmanship.

How Does Your School Rate? Do other schools say, "Yes, you have a great team but you're poor sports!" No one likes to be called a poor sport. What can you do if sportsmanship is a problem at your school? You, the cheerleaders, must teach your student body to be humble in victory, proud in defeat.

How? The first thing to do is to set a good example. Next time you are at a game, notice what the players do. After the game they congratulate each other for a fine game, win or lose. Why not do the same for opposing cheerleaders?

Before the Game. If you are the home team, welcome the visiting cheerleaders as soon as they arrive. Introduce yourselves and ask if they need any help in getting their section organized. You will soon find that they share the same interests and have the same problems that you do.

This pregame meeting will also give you an opportunity to coordinate the cheering for the game. For football this is not too difficult. Since both cheering sections will probably be sitting on opposite sides of the field, you will not disrupt each others' cheers. But in a crowded gymnasium simultaneous cheering can lead to confusion. Establish "ground rules" with the opposing cheerleaders. Decide ahead of time who is to have the first yell at a time-out. One way is to let the visitors yell first during the first and third quarters and have the home team yell first for the second and fourth quarters. Since basketball cheers are generally short, there will usually be enough time for both sides to get in a cheer during a time-out. If a plan is decided on before the game starts, there will not be any misunderstandings.

Another idea you can use is the combined yell. This is done with all cheerleaders in the center of the field or floor. They lead both rooting sections in the same yell at the same time. You have to use a yell that both sides know and all cheerleaders must lead it at the same speed. A little practice together out of sight can help this. Here is an example of a cheer that you could use:

> Two Bits, Four Bits, Six Bits a Dollar!
> Everyone for FOOTBALL, Stand Up and Holler!

By asking both cheering sections to work together on a common project such as the combined yell, you can develop an attitude of friendly competition instead of mutual dislike.

The hello yell before a game is a good way to encourage sportsmanship. The home team usually greets the visitors who reply with a yell.

During the Game. Your cheers during the game should always be designed to build up your own team and never tear down or ridicule your opponent.

At football games never try to drown out the signals of the opposing quarterback. Your own players will resent this as much as the opposing players. They prefer to win the game on their own ability and do not want help from unsportsmanlike conduct.

Never lead a yell when either team is in a huddle. Give a short or one-word yell as your team leaves the huddle and then ask for silence while the signals are called.

At basketball games discourage your rooters from yelling while an opponent is shooting foul shots. This is not only bad manners but rarely has any effect. Stop any booing from your section immediately. If you allow one or two individuals to boo, it will quickly spread through your entire section. If you cannot stop the booing, drown it out with a "big noise" chant.

Frequently, adults are more guilty of booing than students. If this is a problem, train your students to stand up and shout down any booing that starts in your cheering section.

Keep the fans acting like good sports. The team members try exceptionally hard to be good sports and if the student body embarrasses them, it might take some of the steam out of their efforts. Your team should be proud of the way the students behave, and try all the harder as a result.

What if an Opponent Is Injured or Fouls Out? Give him "A Round of Applause and Fifteen Rahs." Show admiration for the way he played; not joy that he must leave the game. And here is a tip on injuries: When a player is lying on the ground, he is probably either stunned or has had the wind knocked out of him. If so, he will not hear you if you cheer for him. Wait until he is on his feet or is helped from the field. If you do not know his name, cheer for him by number or school.

During Halftime. Continue to show good sportsmanship with cheerleader exchanges during the halftime period. Since the teams are in the dressing rooms, your halftime cheering is for fun and to build school spirit.

Go over and lead a yell for the opponent's cheering section while their cheerleaders do a yell for your section. You can also exchange song leaders for musical numbers. But work out all the details of the exchanges at your pregame meeting so that you do not waste valuable minutes at halftime.

After the Game. This will depend on the outcome. If you have lost, you want your students to remain proud of your team and the manner in which they played. But they should not feel bitter toward your opponent. If you have won, express joy and pleasure without ridiculing the other school. If the opposing players show bitterness and act like poor sports, ignore them. You will only damage your own reputation by getting involved.

A number of leagues have adopted the practice of asking all players, coaches, cheerleaders, and song leaders to remain on the field while both alma maters are sung. All participants first stand in front of the losing section while they sing their alma mater, and then they cross to the other side for the alma mater of the victors. Not only is this an effective way to build good sportsmanship among players and students, but it is an excellent way to get the spectators to stay to the end of the game. If this is not done in your league, talk to your coach or principal. Once initiated, this practice has always been popular.

Look upon an athletic contest as something that is supposed to be fun—not as a matter of life or death. The students on the other side of the field or gym are the same age as you and may even live in the same town. Win or lose, you should still be on friendly terms after the game. If you are not, you are taking the game too seriously. Do not ridicule anything or anyone but learn to recognize good-natured fighting spirit.

Good Sportsmanship Is Contagious. If the cheerleaders encourage it, the students will quickly pick it up. If one school really promotes good sportsmanship, it will spread throughout the league. But good sportsmanship on the part of the student body must begin with the cheerleaders. If your students are still known as poor sports at the end of the year, you have no one to blame but yourself.

IV

Your Routines

9

Jump!

And Look Good Doing It!

Think for a moment of pictures you have seen of cheerleaders. Most were probably jumping, as this is the image many people have when they think of cheerleaders.

Jumps should be an important part of all cheerleading routines and they should get special emphasis from you in your practice sessions. Anyone can jump but only someone who has practiced can make jumps look good.

Why are jumps important? When you jump, you oppose the law of gravity for a brief moment. If done well, a jump conveys feelings of joy, exuberance, and accomplishment. A sloppy jump conveys only feelings of confusion and failure.

The time you spend working on your jumps to make them graceful and as high as possible is well spent. Now here are some secrets about jumping to help you make yours good:

PREPARATION AND TAKE-OFF

1. Start with two or three running steps forward, do a small jump to bring your feet together with your knees bent, ready to spring upward for the main jump.

2. Take a deep breath before your first step and hold it until you reach the peak of your jump.

3. Use your arms to help lift yourself into the air. Swing them down and back during the preparation and then bring

them forward and upward quickly as you spring. Once in the air, place your arms in the position for the pose at the peak of your jump.

IN THE AIR

1. To make your jumps look higher, hold your body still at the peak of your jump. This gives the impression of being momentarily suspended in midair. To achieve this, have the pose that you will use as you reach the peak of the jump planned and practiced ahead of time. Practice placing each part of your body in the proper position for the pose while standing still. Then practice the pose while jumping.

2. Look pleasant every time you jump. While concentrating on jumping high, your face may show strain unless you plan an expression ahead of time. Have someone watch while you practice your jumps and tell you when you are not smiling. If you smile on every jump, you will be smiling when pictures are taken of you jumping at the games. Always watch the spectators during a jump. If you do a jump with your body sideways to the spectators, turn and look over your shoulder at them.

3. Here are two exercises you can do standing on the ground that will help you when you do jumps with your legs extended as in a split jump.

a) Practice kicking your legs one at a time in the desired direction, and try to hold your leg in that position for a split second before it comes down.

b) Practice kicking beyond the desired position to stretch the muscles. This will give you a chance to perfect the pose you wish to assume in the air without worrying about the take-off and landing.

4. If you want your arms out or up at the peak of the jump, learn to move them quickly into position without hunching your shoulders. Do not allow a violent motion of the arm to pull your shoulders away from a level position. This will help you keep your balance when you land.

LANDING AND FOLLOW-THROUGH

Your jump is not finished until you make a graceful landing. Even jumps well done will look poor if landed off-balance.

Plan the position you want to land in ahead of time. Let your toes hit the ground first and then press your heels into the ground as you bend your knees. Keep your feet together and land as a compact unit. If you extend your arms down or out to the sides, this will help you balance yourself.

Once you have learned to make good basic landings without losing your balance, you can try some other landings. One example is to land in a crouch with one leg slightly ahead of the other and with your arms at your sides with the fingers straight and pointed to the ground. Another way is to make a low jump and land in a lunge. But do not use specialized landings too often or you will wear them out.

If you want to land on one foot only, extend the other foot during the jump. Bring it to the ground only after you have landed with your full weight on the first foot. There must be a definite interval between the time the feet land or it will appear that you tried a feet-together landing and missed.

After you land, move quickly into another pose, such as standing with your feet together and with your hands on your hips. This does two things: first, if you landed off-balance, you can cover up by moving to a standing pose; second, if you are jumping as a squad and one member jumps poorly, you will still end the yell together and in an organized manner.

MAKE YOUR JUMPS LOOK HIGHER

Here are a few tricks that will make your jumps look higher than they actually are:

1. End the jump in a low position, such as a crouch or knee bend. This puts a lot of space between the peak of the jump and the landing, making the jump look higher.

2. Hold your arms low at the peak of the jump. This might be difficult at first but it is effective.

3. On some jumps, try bending your knees at the peak of

the jump to draw your legs up under you. This puts space between you and the ground.

4. Keep your head as well as the rest of your body perfectly still at the top of the jump and you will seem to remain in the air longer.

The best way to make your jumps look high is to have a smooth preparation, a graceful take-off, a motionless pose at the peak of the jump, and a landing with perfect balance. A jump done well always looks higher than a sloppy one.

WHEN AND HOW TO USE JUMPS

The best way to use a jump is to emphasize a single word in a yell, usually the last one. This will give a final climax to your yell. Jumps can also be effective within the routines if carefully planned. A common method is on spellouts or countdowns. The cheerleaders can jump individually or together on each letter or number. But on spellouts, train the students to yell as you land, not at the peak of the jump as you would for single words at the end of fight yells. This gives the students a chance to take a breath during the jump so that they will be ready to shout on the landing.

All of your cheers should have a definite ending. Cheerleaders can spoil the effect of cheers without realizing it by running the end of the yell into the general applause and shouting that follows the yell. This mistake is easy to make because you usually jump on the last word of the cheer as well as after the cheer is over. End your yell with a definite pose. Then you can lead the students in applause and shouting. If you want to jump at random, do it as an expression of joy and enthusiasm following a score, good plays, or successful cheers.

For variety, you can put jumps together in groups of two or three. Experiment with the ones you do best, putting them together until you hit on a combination that feels comfortable and is easy to do. Use the landing of one jump as the take-off for the next. You can try using a series of different jumps or you can repeat the same jump using different arm positions. Plan a definite position for the arms between each jump.

Do not get carried away on group jumping. It is hard enough to get a cheerleading team to stay together on one jump. You will have to put in a lot of practice to make a series of jumps look good.

JUMPING AND YOUR UNIFORM

Practice some jumps in your uniform. This will tell you ahead of time if it can take the strain. Otherwise, your first jump at a rally or game may be your last. You should have confidence in your uniform and know that it will stay together, look good, and feel comfortable while jumping.

BASIC JUMPS YOU CAN USE

There are many different ways to jump. Some are easy, others are more difficult. A simple jump done well is more useful and effective than a fancy jump done poorly. Apply the general rules that have been mentioned to the following jumps and select the ones you like and do best.

Standard Split. A common but spectacular jump is the split jump. Once you are in the air, spread your feet apart as far as you can. Keep your knees as straight as possible but get your feet back together for the landing.

To help keep your balance on low split jumps, your feet should go directly out to the sides, but you can put your arms in nearly any position.

On high split jumps, bring your feet slightly forward and keep your arms below shoulder level at the peak of the jump.

Bent Split. Split jumps can be done with one knee bent. The beautiful stag jump is nothing more than a split jump in which you bend one leg at the knee so that the foot touches the knee of the trailing leg when you are at the peak of the jump. This can be a dangerous jump if you cannot get your feet back together for the landing.

Straight Jump. On the straight jump, you merely spring into the air with the feet together and land with them together. At the peak of the jump, you can straighten your legs or draw them up under you. You will find a variety of attractive hand positions for straight jumps. Practice with a mirror or with others watching you to determine the hand and arm positions that look best for your squad.

One way to change the straight jump is to start with your arms pointing to the right, then bend your knees and tuck your feet under you as you jump. At the peak of the jump, twist both knees to the right and quickly bring both arms to the front. Bring the knees back to the front and the arms back to the right side for the landing.

Back Jump. The back jump is similar to the straight jump. It is done by arching your back, throwing your hands back over your head, and bringing your feet up behind you. A good back jump will look like a capital "C."

On preparation for the jump, bring your arms forward and then explode into the air, swinging your arms up and over your head until they nearly touch your feet. This jump looks best when done sideways to the spectators. You can either have your feet together or apart.

Another arm motion that can be used on this jump is to swing them straight in front of you and at the peak of the jump, pull your elbows back behind you.

SUMMARY OF JUMPING

To see yourself as others see you when you are jumping, practice in front of a mirror. Do not give up on a jump just because it looks sloppy when you first try it. Practice it a while and give yourself a chance to learn it. Apply the basic jumping rules listed in this chapter each time you practice. If you start working on your jumps early, you will be a jumping cheerleader at the first game!

10

Creating Your Own Cheers and Routines

Your new cheers should be fun to say and easy to understand. Choose words that are understandable, and put definite motions to them. Try to have something different in each yell to make it distinctive but be careful about getting too tricky or complicated. The students have to feel confident that they know when to yell or they will not yell at all in order to avoid the embarrassment of yelling at the wrong time.

Introduce new yells gradually and do not ask your student body to memorize a complete set of new yells each season. Save some of your new yells for later when they can be used to pep up your repertoire.

Do not expect an overwhelming response to a new yell right away. People usually have to see and hear something several times before they will fully participate in the cheer. At first, they are watching and listening. Only after the cheer is learned and practiced will the student body fully participate in a new cheer.

If one of your new yells is not working well, check it against the rules for good yells that are explained in the following chapter. If the yell still seems to be a good one, then the cause of the problem is probably minor. Before dropping the yell, try to find out what is wrong with it. It might be that the

86

rhythm is too fast or too slow or maybe it needs a longer pause in a certain place. Perhaps the motion for one of the words is confusing or maybe some squad members are not doing a certain motion at exactly the same time as the others. Maybe you are asking for the cheer at the wrong psychological moment.

When creating a new cheer, choose the words first and then fit appropriate motions to them. The following sections will give you information on selecting words and putting them together to make a yell, and give you suggestions on choosing effective motions for your cheers.

Words: How to Choose and Arrange Them

The following will give you information on making up cheers. Specific suggestions for making up novelty yells, chants, spellouts, and longer cheers will be mentioned later.

FIRST: DECIDE ON PURPOSE
Before working on the words for your cheer, ask yourself, what is its purpose? How will it be used at the game? Then classify it as one of the following: fight, special purpose, school-spirit, or novelty yell.

SECOND: SELECT WORDS
Make a list of words and short phrases that are appropriate for the purpose of your cheer. For example, if you are making up a school-spirit yell, you would list such words as spirit, proud, best, glory, etc.

When your list is completed, go over it and eliminate any words that have more than two syllables. Long, complicated words rarely sound good when yelled by the cheering section.

Then cross out any words that could be classified as primitive, such as "kill 'em, tear 'em apart!" These words can still be found in yells at some schools. There are good reasons for avoiding them. Controlling the students is a difficult task.

If you teach cheers which bring out primitive instincts, you can turn your organized cheering section into a disorderly mob. There are so many good words that will convey the idea of your cheer that you should not have to resort to crude ones.

One of your jobs is to build a favorable sportsmanship reputation for your school. Yells that are in poor taste do not help. An old favorite, "Give 'em the Ax!" falls into this category and has been discontinued at many schools. If your school has a traditional cheer of this nature, do not drop it all at once. Fade it out gradually and replace it with new and interesting cheers that serve the same purpose.

Now read the words on your list aloud. Remove any that sound like other words, such as "faith-face" and "clash-crash." Also take out any with a double meaning, such as "Cheer for the White and *Green Team*." This yell could be misunderstood since "green team" is a phrase often used to describe an inexperienced team.

Choose words that are clear and sharp when yelled by the crowd. Your main goal is to inspire the team through the cheering section. You are wasting the efforts of the cheering section if you use words not understandable to the athletes.

The following list of suggested words for all kinds of cheers are words that rhyme, which should help you when you are working on rhyming cheers.

WORD CHART

School-Spirit Words

TEAM: beam, steam, dream, scream
FAME: game, same, aim, tame, train
TRUE: blue, new, pull through
FANS: stands, grand, land, hand, man, can
BEST: test, all the rest, in the West
PROUDER: louder (proudly, loudly)
GLORY: story
BELIEVE: achieve, succeed
SPIRIT: hear it

Other school-spirit words: pep, jump, active, honor, school, success, victory, onward

Time and Place Words

NOW: down, how, town, touchdown, vow, wow
TONIGHT: fight, might, right, dynamite
TODAY: hooray, play, way, say
THERE: where, fair, square
AGAIN: men, ten, end
STRAIGHT: eight, bait, gate
DOWN: around, bound, sound, ground
    Other time and place words: soon, quick, here, field, floor

Words to Describe Your Team

BOLD: told
FINE: line, nine
SMART: part, start
ON THE BEAM: team
ON THEIR TOES: goes, knows
FAIR: square, there, where
STEAM: team, beam, dream, scream
SPEED: lead, defeat, neat, feet, beat
MEN: again, end, ten
STRONG: along, can't go wrong
HOT: got, lot
TOUGH: rough, enough, bluff, stuff
    Other words to describe your team: brave, energy, swift, alert, eager, big, quick, sharp, might, courage, fierce, powerful, got what it takes

Words to Describe What the Students Want and What the Team Does

DEFEAT (opponent): feet, beat, neat, lead, speed
DOMINATE: straight
GO: foe, so, low, toe, to and fro, know, throw, hello, hi-ho, hold
FIGHT: dynamite, right, tonight, might
WIN: begin, thick or thin, in
BEAT: neat, keep
SCORE: more, four, floor, for, roar
HOLD: bold, mold, cold
STRIKE: excite
GOAL: roll, toll
DRIVE: alive, strive

CHARGE: large
GET ON THE BALL: all, fall, call
KICK: quick
ARROW: no, blow, show, foe, owe
Other words to describe what the students want and what the team does: pass, run, force, finish, challenge, control, stop, harder, action, victory, master, gain, halt, point, basket, touchdown, play, move

Words that Describe What the Students Do
SHOUT: out, doubt, about
CHEER: here, hear, year, near, clear
YELL: swell
SCREAM: team, beam, dream
CALL: all, fall, ball
NOISE: poise, boys
LOUD: proud
SAY: way, stay, play, hey
Other words that describe what the students do: roar, cry, chant

Words that Rhyme with Numbers
ONE: won, begun
TWO: blue, true, new
THREE: see
FOUR: more, score, floor, for, roar
FIVE: alive
SIX: mix, fix, kicks
SEVEN: heaven
EIGHT: straight, bait, gate
NINE: fine, line
TEN: again, end, men

Words that Rhyme with Colors
WHITE: fight, tonight, dynamite, might, right
RED: said
BLUE: you, do, too, two, new, true, pull through
GREEN: team, steam, on the beam
GOLD: hold, bold, told, sold
BLACK: back
GRAY: hey, stay, play

THIRD: PUTTING THE CHEER TOGETHER

You are now ready to build a cheer choosing from the words remaining on your list. Do not get carried away at this point and make the cheer into something else than was originally intended. If it was supposed to be a short yell, keep it that way. Do not let it grow into a novelty production.

Rhythm is what holds the cheer together, whether it is a short cheer or a long one. In addition to the basic rhythm, some cheers are held together by rhyme. Although all good cheers will have a definite rhythm, not all cheers need to rhyme.

Starting on page 92 you will find examples of specific types of yells with the rhythmical system explained for each. You will also find a section explaining the basic systems of rhyme and instructions for using it correctly and effectively. Before starting to work on your own yell, read over those that are similar in type to the one you are planning to create. This will help you to get a feeling for the yells and how to write them.

Arrange the words so that the yell is easy to say, sharp-sounding, and rhythmical. Put breathing spaces before any major words you want emphasized.

Allow for the echo when using especially loud words. Put a pause between the loud words to let the echo fade away. This sounds good and the students will be impressed with the echo they made as well as having time to take a breath.

Avoid putting like-sounding words together, such as, "The Bears *Are Our* Team!" Cheers should end with a strong one-syllable word or a series of one-syllable words separated by breathing spaces. As you make up the cheer, say it over to yourself and exaggerate the rhythm so that it is similar to the way it will sound when yelled by a crowd. Will it be understandable?

Most cheers have the same rhythmical speed from beginning to end, but not all cheers need to be this way. You can add variety by starting slowly and speeding up. An example of a change of rhythm is the spellout that is done faster each time the word is spelled. Do not overuse changes in rhythm during cheers. Save them for your novelty yells and chants.

How to Use the Charts

The following charts illustrate some of the more common rhythm patterns for cheers. You will find it easy to adapt your own words to these patterns. Read the following directions first:

1. The words are first yelled at normal volume, then louder, and on the last cheer, very loud. Here is an example:

Fight!   (normal)

FIGHT! (louder)

FIGHT! (very loud)

2. Words, letters, groups of words, claps, and pauses are separated into columns by spaces. Everything within a column is done to one beat of rhythm.

3. Clapping, sound effects, and pauses are interchangeable in many cases and may be substituted as you prefer.

4. The sound is carried over two or more beats when letters are repeated, as in "Whoooooooooooooop!"

SPIRIT CHEERS

Section 1.   School Initials, Slogans, and Colors

The following cheers are all based on a simple four-count rhythm for each line. This is the basic structure for many cheers. They depend almost entirely on rhythm for their effect and do not necessarily need to rhyme. Some of the cheers have an additional word added to the end of the yell. This puts special emphasis on the end of the cheer and usually adds to its effectiveness.

You can use these examples for your school by changing the initials, colors, or mascot.

Initials

L	H	S	*(pause)*
L	H	S	*(pause)*
L	*(pause)*	*(pause)*	*(pause)*
H	*(pause)*	*(pause)*	*(pause)*
S	*(pause)*	*(pause)*	THE

BEST!

C	H	S	*(pause)*
C	H	S	*(pause)*
CAScade	*(pause)*	HIGH	*(pause)*
SCHOOL!	*(pause)*	(CLAP)	(CLAP)
FIGHT!			

Color-Slogan Combinations

Blue	*(pause)*	White	*(pause)*
C'mon	let's	FIGHT!	*(pause)*
(CLAP)	(CLAP)	Blue	*(pause)*
(CLAP)	(CLAP)	White	*(pause)*
Come	on	team	*(pause)*
(CLAP)	(CLAP)	**FIGHT!**	

RED	*(pause)*	WHITE	*(pause)*
GET	THAT	BALL!	*(pause)*
(CLAP)	(CLAP)	RED	*(pause)*
(CLAP)	(CLAP)	WHITE	*(pause)*
GET	*(pause)*	THAT	*(pause)*
BALL!			

Gold	*(pause)*	Blue	*(pause)*
We're	for	You.	*(pause)*
Gold!	Gold!	Blue!	Blue!
THAT'S	**OUR**	SCHOOL!	

Short Sentences *(usually rhyme by repeating same word)*

WE'RE	THE	BEST!	*(pause)*
WE'RE	THE	BEST!	*(pause)*
WE'RE	*(pause)*	*(pause)*	*(pause)*
THE	*(pause)*	*(pause)*	*(pause)*
BEST!			

Black	*(pause)*	Hawks	*(pause)*
They're	the	Best.	*(pause)*
Black	*(pause)*	Hawks	*(pause)*
They're	the	Best.	*(pause)*
Black	Hawks	Black	Hawks
(pause)	They're the	**BEST!**	

Longer Sentences *(usually combined with clapping to help maintain a good rhythm, and always rhyme)*

ALL of us	HERE are	HUSky	FANS!
(CLAPclap)	(CLAPclap)	(CLAPclap)	(CLAP)
WE'VE got the	BEST team	IN the	LAND!
(CLAPclap)	(CLAPclap)	(CLAPclap)	(CLAP)

The TIGERS	ARE	the BEST!	*(pause)*
(clap)	(clap)	(clapCLAP)	*(pause)*
BETTER	than ALL	the REST!	*(pause)*
(clap)	(clap)	(clapCLAP)	*(pause)*
The TIGERS	*(pause)*	ARE	*(pause)*
the **BEST!**			

Section 2. Spellouts

Spellouts are one of the easiest types of yells to create. They can be used for your school name, the coach's name, words that are descriptive of a group, such as TEAM or words that describe an attitude, such as BEST.

Some have a regular rhythm and uniform length of line, but not all spellouts must be that way in order to be effective. You can change the number of beats in each line if this is necessary without hindering the rhythmical feeling of the cheer.

Spell the word just once if there is any chance of confusion as to what you are spelling. The major offender, of course, is H-E-L-L-O-H-E-L-L-O. Or was it O-H-E-L-L?

If the word is suitable for spelling several times, use rhythm changes to separate each spellout: B—R—U—I—N—S; (faster) B-R-U-I-N-S; (fast) B R U I N S; BRUINS!

You can also use volume changes to separate the spellouts: B-R-U-I-N-S; (soft) b-r-u-i-n-s; (loud) B R U I N S; **BRUINS!** After the spellout is completed, say the word that you have spelled.

Basic Methods. Here are two examples of simple spellouts using one word. They have the same number of beats in each line within the cheer:

T	*(pause)*	E	*(pause)*	A	M	*(pause)*
T	*(pause)*	E	*(pause)*	A	M	*(pause)*
T	E	A	M	*(pause)*	*(pause)*	**TEAM!**

F	*(pause)*	I	*(pause)*	G	H	T	*(pause)*
F	*(pause)*	I	*(pause)*	G	H	T	*(pause)*
F	I	G	H	T	*(pause)*	*(pause)*	**FIGHT!**

Here is an example of a simple one-word spellout in which the number of beats in the last three lines is different from that in the first two lines:

Gimme-a	T	*(pause)*	E	*(pause)*	A *(pause)*	M
That's-right-a	T	*(pause)*	E	*(pause)*	A *(pause)*	M
(pause)	T	E	A	M		
(pause)	T	E	A	M		
(pause)	(CLAP)	(CLAP)	(CLAP)	(CLAP)		
TEAM!						

Adding Novelty Effects. This yell is a simple one-word spell-out in which the rhythm gradually gets faster. The first line is slow, the second line is a little faster, and the final spellout is fast.

T	Rah!	E	Rah!	A—M	Rah!
T	Rah!	E	Rah!	A—M	Rah!
T	E	A	M	*(pause)*	*(pause)*
RAH!					

Sound effects can be used in spellouts effectively to control the length of the pauses. In a cheer such as this one with long pauses between the letters, clapping is used to control the rhythm.

T	(CLAP)	(CLAP)	(CLAPCLAP)
E	(CLAP)	(CLAP)	(CLAPCLAP)
A	(CLAP)	(CLAP)	(CLAPCLAP)
M	(CLAP)	(CLAP)	(CLAPCLAP)
T	E	A	M
(CLAP)	(CLAP)	(CLAP)	(CLAP)
TEAM!			

Here is a fancier spellout. It uses clapping in addition to pauses between words and it includes a short phrase to introduce each spellout. It starts at normal volume and gets louder throughout the first three lines. The fourth line starts at normal volume and builds up until it is very loud at the end of the cheer.

	We've got the	S	*(pause)*	P	*(pause)*	I-R	I	T
(Louder)	We've got the	S	*(pause)*	P	*(pause)*	I-R	I	T
(LOUD!)	We've got the	S	*(pause)*	P	*(pause)*	I-R	I	T
	We've got the Spirit!	*(pause)*	(CLAP)	*(pause)*	(CLAP)	*(pause)*	(CLAP)	
	We've got the Spirit!	*(pause)*	(CLAP)	*(pause)*	(CLAP)	*(pause)*	(CLAP)	
	WE'VE	*(pause)*	**GOT**	*(pause)*	**SPIRIT!**			

Here is an example of how you can combine a spellout with a slogan. Note that the first line (the spellout) is ten beats long. The next three lines (the slogan) are four beats each. The cheer finishes with a five-beat line.

L	*(pause)*	I	*(pause)*	O	*(pause)*	N	*(pause)*	S	*(pause)*
They're the	BEST!	*(pause)*	*(pause)*						
They're the	BEST!	*(pause)*	*(pause)*						
They're the	BEST!	*(pause)*	*(pause)*						
LIONS,	*(pause)*	*(pause)*	THE	**BEST!**					

("We're THE **BEST**" could also be used.)

Spelling Out Long Words

The next two cheers are examples of spellouts of long or complicated school names. This type of yell is usually done at a slower speed than a yell using short words. If you try to spell a long word too fast, the students will lose the rhythm and it will be difficult to get them to end together. The number of beats in each line will vary depending on the length of the words. Your cheer will sound better if you say the word twice at the end.

Q	*(pause)*	U	*(pause)*	E	*(pause)*	E	*(pause)*	N	*(pause)*
A	*(pause)*	N	*(pause)*	N	*(pause)*	E	*(pause)*		
QUEEN ANNE	*(pause)*	**QUEEN**	**ANNE**	*(pause)*	**FIGHT!**				

Gimme	S	*(pause)*	O	*(pause)*	U		*(pause)*	T-H	*(pause)*	
Add-a	V	*(pause)*	A	*(pause)*	L		*(pause)*	L	E	Y *(pause)*
S	O	U	T	H	*(pause)*					
V	A	L	L	E	Y					
(pause)	*(pause)*	**SOUTH**	**VALLEY!**	*(pause)*	*(pause)*	**SOUTH**	**VALLEY!**			

FIGHT CHEERS

The best fight cheers are made up of a series of short lines, usually with four beats per line. They use a lot of pauses and clapping to add to the rhythmical feeling and effectiveness of the cheer. They are designed to be yelled loudly from the beginning to the end and finish with a powerful word.

Fight cheers do not have to rhyme and they are usually more effective if they have one or two words following the last line. Here are some examples:

GO!	(CLAP)	(CLAP)	(CLAP)
FIGHT!	(CLAP)	(CLAP)	(CLAP)
WIN!	(CLAP)	(CLAP)	(CLAP)
TONIGHT!	(CLAP)	(CLAP)	(CLAP)
GO!	FIGHT!	WIN!	TONIGHT!
(CLAP)	(CLAP)	(CLAP)	(CLAP)
FIGHT!			

LET'S	GO!	(CLAP)	(CLAP)
LET'S	FIGHT!	(CLAP)	(CLAP)
LET'S	WIN!	(CLAP)	(CLAP)
LET'S	GO,	LET'S	FIGHT,
LET'S	WIN,	(CLAP)	(CLAP)
TONIGHT!			

Get	HOT!	*(pause)*	*(pause)*
Get	HOT!	*(pause)*	*(pause)*
Get	HOT	*(pause)*	and WIN
THIS	GAME!	*(pause)*	*(pause)*
Let's	FIGHT!	*(pause)*	*(pause)*
Let's	FIGHT!	*(pause)*	*(pause)*
Let's	FIGHT	*(pause)*	and WIN
THIS	GAME	*(pause)*	*(pause)*
RIGHT	**NOW!**		

Let's	GO!	*(pause)*	*(pause)*
Let's	GO!	*(pause)*	*(pause)*
Let's	GO!	*(pause)*	and GET
THOSE	BEARS!	*(pause)*	*(pause)*
Right	NOW!	*(pause)*	*(pause)*
Right	NOW!	*(pause)*	*(pause)*
Right	NOW!	*(pause)*	GET
THOSE	BEARS!	*(pause)*	*(pause)*
GO	**GET'EM!**		

GO	Huskies	GO!	*(pause)*
FIGHT	Huskies	FIGHT!	*(pause)*
BEAT'EM	Huskies	BEAT'EM!	*(pause)*
GO!	*(pause)*	FIGHT!	*(pause)*
BEAT'EM!	*(pause)*	*(pause)*	TO-
NIGHT!			

GO!	*(pause)*	GO!	*(pause)*
FIGHT!	*(pause)*	FIGHT!	*(pause)*
BEAT'EM!	*(pause)*	BEAT'EM!	*(pause)*
GO	GO	FIGHT	FIGHT
(CLAP)	(CLAP)	**BEAT'EM!**	

Four-beat lines are not an absolute requirement for effective fight cheers. The next one has four beats in the first and third lines, three beats in the second and fourth lines, and four beats in the last two lines.

Black	*(pause)*	White	*(pause)*
Fight!	Fight!	*(pause)*	
Black	*(pause)*	White	*(pause)*
Fight!	Fight!	*(pause)*	
BLACK	BLACK	WHITE	WHITE
(pause)	*(pause)*	**FIGHT!**	**FIGHT!**

If you are planning a fight yell with one or two longer phrases or sentences, use pauses and clapping to help maintain the rhythm.

Yells of this type sound best if you add a line in which the speed and volume is increased after you have said the main sentence. Here are two examples:

	Go *(pause)*	get'em *(pause)*	RIGHT	NOW! *(pause)*	
	Go *(pause)*	get'em *(pause)*	RIGHT	NOW! *(pause)*	
(faster & louder)	Go Go	Go	Go *(pause)*	*(pause)* **RIGHT**	
	NOW!				

GET	TOUGH, YOU	COUGARS *(pause)*		
WE	WILL	WIN	TO-	DAY! *(pause) (pause)*
FIGHT HARD,	YOU	COUGARS *(pause)*		
WE	ARE	HERE TO	STAY! *(pause) (pause)*	
(faster & louder)	**YAYYYYYYYYYYYYYYYYYYYYY**	**COUGARS!**		

NOVELTY YELLS AND SPECIAL EFFECTS

There are many ways to add interest to your repertoire of cheers by using unusual or novelty effects. Here are a few ideas:

Make	that	score!	*(pause)*	rrrrrr	i g h t	now!	*(pause)*	
We	want	more!	*(pause)*	rrrrrr	i g h t	now!	*(pause)*	
SCORE! (CLAP)	(CLAP)	(CLAP)		SCORE! (CLAP)	(CLAP)	(CLAP)		
Sssssscorrrrrrrrrrrrrrrrrrrrrrrrrrrre				**NOW!**				

	WE'RE the	BEST! *(pause)*	t-h-a-t-'-s- - -	RIGHT! *(pause)*
	WE'RE the	BEST *(pause)*	t-o-o-o-o-o- - -	NIGHT! *(pause)*
(ending 1)	*(pause)*	**SO**	**FIGHT!**	
(ending 2)	GO	*(pause)* TIGERS! *(pause)*	(CLAP) (CLAP)	**FIGHT!**

You can also use weird noises, such as animal calls and sounds like, "ZZZZZZZZZZZ, SSSSSSSSSSSS," or even "OOOOOOOOOOOO." Try clapping and foot-stamping sequences and use odd-sounding words like "Whoop!"

The drummers in your band can help you with special sound effects:

(DRUM)	(DRUM)	(DRUM)	(DRUM)	
GO	Huskies	GO!	*(pause)*	
(DRUM)	(DRUM)	(DRUM)	(DRUM)	
FIGHT	Huskies	FIGHT!	*(pause)*	
GO	Huskies	GO!	*(pause)*	
FIGHT	Huskies	FIGHT!	*(pause)*	
go	Go	GO	**GO**	(drum beats on each of these
HUSKIES!	(with drum beat)			counts, gradually get louder)

Special Endings. Finish your yell with an unusual pose, such as a clawing bear or an Indian hunter. Accompany the pose with appropriate sounds.

GO	Huskies	GO!	*(pause)*
FIGHT	Huskies	FIGHT!	*(pause)*
GO	Huskies	FIGHT	Huskies
GO	FIGHT	*(pause)*	*(pause)*

MUSH! (or growl, school mascot sound, animal noise, etc.)

Other ways to finish yells include pyramids and tumbling stunts. (*Note:* Tumbling stunts can be very effective in cheerleading. However, the authors feel that tumbling is difficult and dangerous to try to learn from a book. For those who wish to learn tumbling, we recommend instruction from a recognized tumbling authority or gymnastics coach.)

Catchy Phrases. You can refer to your opponent in an amusing way, such as in this next cheer:

WE	WANT	*(pause)*	*(pause)*		
WE	WANT	*(pause)*	*(pause)*		
A	Bearrrrrrrrrrrr	RUG!			
THAT'S	RIGHT!	*(pause)*	*(pause)*		
THAT'S	RIGHT!	*(pause)*	*(pause)*		
A	Bearrrrrrrrrrrr	RUG!			
(pause)	*(pause)*	**TO-**	**DAY!**	(or **Tonight**)	

Other examples: Beaver Tail, Tiger Tail, Indian Feather, Bulldog Tooth, Pirate Gold, etc.

You can also use catchy phrases that are popular at your school, such as "Cool" or "Way to Go."

One-Word Cheers. A good cheer can be made up using just one word if the word can be adapted to sound like a sound effect. Beavers has two syllables. (Other two-syllable words, names, or mascots could be used.)

BEA-	VERS!	(CLAP)	(CLAP)	BEA-	VERS!	(CLAP)	(CLAP)

BeeeeeeeeeeeeeeeVERRRRRRRSSSSSSSSSSSSSSS *(pause)* (CLAP) (CLAP)
BeeeeeeeeeeeeeeeVERRRRRRRSSSSSSSSSSSSSSS *(pause)* (CLAP) (CLAP)
BEAVERS!

Props and Motions. Special props, such as small pom poms or pennants can be used by the cheerleaders, the pep club or the whole cheering section. You should also consider using physical actions on the part of your rooters, like throwing the fist, standing up, or leaning from side to side.

Systems of Rhyme

The numbers at the left identify the rhyming lines. Lines with the same number will rhyme with one another.

A *Best for short chants but can also be used for longer yells.*

1 SCORE! SCORE!   We gotta WIN, We gotta WIN,
                          1 We gotta WIN TONIGHT!
1 We want MORE!   We gotta WIN, We gotta WIN,
                          1 We gotta WIN SO FIGHT!

1 Let's raise that score,
2 Let's GO,
2 Let's GO!

B *These are the easiest to make up for longer yells. This system is the most common.*

1	That's O.K.,	1	Pep it up, step it up,	1	Let's GO!
2	That's all right	2	Fight, fight, fight!	2	Let's FIGHT!
3	So get in there	3	We're for [your school]	3	Let's WIN
2	And FIGHT!	2	That's RIGHT!	2	TONIGHT!

1 Hey, gang,
2 Whatta you say?
3 We can beat the [opponent]
2 Any old day!

C *These can be easily speeded up and are good for long chants.*

1	Fight, fight,	1	Hey, hey,
1	With all your might.	1	Whatta you say?
2	Come on team,	2	Let's push 'em back
1	Let's win tonight!	1	The other way!

D *This is for longer yells where the final line is a summary of the other three.*

1 Let's go, big team, let's go!
2 Let's fight, big team, let's fight!
3 Let's win, big team, let's win!
3 Let's go, let's fight, let's win!

E *This is a simple system for longer yells.*

1 Center, end, tackle, guard
1 Work together, hit 'em hard!
2 Hit 'em high, hit 'em low,
2 Come on team, let's go!

F *This is a good system for syncopated yells or yells with different rhythms.*

1 Go, Huskies, go!
2 Fight, Huskies, fight!
1 We all know
2 You'll win tonight!

Rules of Rhyme

1. Either keep each line or sentence about the same length or else use short lines and long lines and match them by size. For example, start with a short line, then use two long lines followed by a short line on the end. You can also use short lines for the first and third lines and long lines for the second and fourth.

2. Do not end every line with a rhyming word. This produces weak, singsong cheers. Refer to the chart for examples of rhyming systems that are effective.

3. Rhyming should not attract attention to itself. Base your rhymes on sound, not spelling, although spelling can be a guide.

4. When using words that rhyme, try for one-syllable words. If you want to rhyme two-syllable words, try to make both syllables rhyme. "Louder" and "prouder" rhyme better than "louder" and "taller" because both syllables rhyme.

Another way to make your rhymes stronger is to rhyme two words near the end of the rhyming lines. An example is, "Let's give a yell for the *green* and *white,* and clap and cheer for our *team tonight.*"

How to Choose the Right Motions and Positions

The motions for your cheers accomplish two purposes. They help the students say the cheer in the desired manner and they also help to convey the idea and meaning of the cheer. The motions support the words. This is why the words are made up first and then the motions added to them.

GUIDE FOR MATCHING MOTIONS AND WORDS

1. Motions Should Be Descriptive of the Sound You Want from the Students

Choose motions that will guide the students in saying the cheer. Use novelty stunts and cute motions only when they perform this function.

You will have more control over the students if you use different kinds of motions for each type of sound you want. Here are some suggestions:

To get a quick, loud burst of sound from the students, use quick sharp motions.

To increase the volume of the sound, use a continuous, circular motion that starts small and gets bigger; or use one that starts low to the ground and rises to an overhead position. A motion that starts with the arms in a down position and slowly rises is often used.

To increase the speed of a phrase, repeat a motion or series of motions over and over and gradually increase the speed. Use a series of motions that you can do equally well at slow or fast speeds. If you speed up the students with a motion that you cannot do fast, they will run away from you.

To increase the speed and the volume at the same time, combine the motions for increased speed and volume together by gradually raising the arms up and simultaneously increasing the speed of the motions. You can lean forward and rotate your hands about each other, slowly at first, and then bring the arms up and rotate the hands faster and faster.

2. Motions Should Be Descriptive of the Words

If you have directional words, such as "up-down," "right-left," or phrases like "raise that score," the motion should be in the appropriate direction. (On "right" or "left," the cheerleaders must make the motion in the opposite direction so that it will correspond with the students' right or left.)

Words that are emphasized, such as "go" "fight" "to-

night," should have motions with a lot of body movement. The motion may use both arms and a kick, lunge, or jump. Contrast these big, whole-body motions with others, using less body movement during sentences, phrases, and words that are not emphasized. The motions for a less important phrase, for example, might be done completely with just one arm.

On words that imply force, such as "fight," do the motion with force. Make the position a strong one, such as lunging at the students with a clenched fist. On short, simple yells, keep the motions simple, too. Avoid getting involved in fancy maneuvers when the students are only saying a few emphasized words.

The style of the motion should fit the nature of the word. For example, the motion for the word "smoothly" would be quite different from the motion for the word "quickly."

3. Motions and Pauses Between Words Should Emphasize the Rhythmical Pattern of the Cheer

Use one definite, specific motion for each main beat of the yell and each emphasized word. Do not run several motions together during one emphasized word or syllable. On "Let's Go Big Team, Let's FIGHT!" the final word gets just one sharp motion.

Make your motions fit the length of the words and phrases. One-syllable words and short phrases that are said rapidly get just one motion. For two-syllable words and longer phrases, use a series of motions. Use the words and syllables that are not emphasized as stepping stones to help you blend together the main motions of the cheer.

If you have a series of emphasized syllables or words that seem to require a main motion for each beat, use outward or extended motions for the odd-numbered beats and inward or contracted motions for the even-numbered beats. The rhythm is "Out—In—Out—In."

Remember that the purpose of the motions is to help the students say the yell together. If you use just one motion for a group of emphasized words or if you use several big motions during a single word or syllable, the students will find it difficult to follow you.

All good cheers have pauses so that the students can take a breath. It is important that you do specific motions during the pauses so that they will know exactly when to yell the next word. The motions should be simple and emphasize the basic rhythm of the cheer. During pauses, a preparatory motion such as a windup or a couple of steps forward can be used. A preparatory motion is particularly effective just before the last word of the cheer and will help you give it emphasis. Time your movements during pauses so that the emphasized word will be at the peak of a jump or at the end of a motion.

You can also use clapping and sound effects to control the length of pauses. Clapping should have a definite and controllable rhythm or it will become just noise. Establish a specific number of claps to be done in rapid succession.

If you put long pauses between claps, you will have the problem of controlling the length of *that* pause, too. Have the students clap along with you on some of the cheers.

When using sound effects to fill pauses, your band can be a big help. As musicians, they have been trained to maintain a given rhythm and they can do it consistently.

4. Motions Should Be Consistent with the Style and Meaning of the Cheer

Your repertoire will include different yells for different purposes. Match the style of your routine to the purpose of the yell. Otherwise, your cheers will look the same whether they are fight yells, spirit yells, or novelty numbers.

A highly rhythmical fight yell with strong sounding words

will look best with stiff arm positions and powerful motions. School-spirit and novelty yells are more flexible and in these areas you can express your personality.

Your job in leading the students is easier on traditional yells and songs that they know well. For these you can use a different variety of motions and work in some of your novelty and gymnastic stunts.

WAYS TO MAKE YOUR JOB EASIER
1. Adding Variety Without Adding Difficulty

There are several shortcuts you can use when you need a new cheer in a hurry or you want to freshen up an old one. Try some of the following systems if you have limited time in which to work out a new cheer or make improvements in an old one. They will make the motions more interesting without adding to the number of new things the squad must learn.

Rotation. The motion moves down the line as each squad member does it in turn.

Opposite. The motion is done at the same time but half of the squad goes one way and the rest go in the opposite direction.

Alternate. The motion is done alternately by every other member in the line.

Position Change / Body Change. The same motion is done from a different position, such as standing up the first time and then doing the motion while crouching.

Formation Change. The same motion is done in a different formation.

When using any of these systems, plan your routine so that there is a definite pose both before and after the sequence so that the team can start and end together.

2. Simplifying Chants

Develop a few standard sets of motions that will fit a large variety of chants. One set of three-beat motions can be used for all three-beat chants, such as "Get that Ball!" or "Hold that Line!" You should also have a set of four-beat motions for four-beat chants, etc. Using this method, you can make up a chant at the game and have appropriate motions ready instantly. You can change the motions in each category from time to time to keep them fresh and interesting.

FINAL CHECK

Once you have completed your routine for the new cheer, check it over. Are most of the motions easy to learn? Do the motions help you get the students to yell together? Do they get the type of sound from the students that you want? Are the motions logical? Do they fit in with the nature of the cheer? Do they convey its purpose and feeling?

If you answered "yes" to the above questions, your cheer is ready for the final finishing touches. Now is the time for the squad to rehearse it together and perfect it.

How to Make Motions Look Good

The manner in which you do your motions is as important as choosing the right motions in the first place.

Your motions should always look neat and clear-cut. If they appear effortless, the students will feel confident and enthusiastic. But you will convey a feeling of fatigue if your motions appear to be hard work for you. Here are a few suggestions that will help you make your motions look easy, snappy, and enthusiastic:

1. Get each squad member to learn each motion the exact way it is to be done so that he will practice the moves correctly. If errors are not corrected early, they may become habits that are difficult to break.

2. Feel the rhythm of the cheer in your head and keep your mind one motion ahead of your body. This will help you with your timing so that you do the proper motion at the exact moment it should be done.

3. Project your motions to the students by exaggerating them just as you can project your voice with a megaphone. Most of the students are some distance from you. A motion that might seem slightly overdone to you will usually look just right at a distance.

4. Practice your motions until you can move swiftly from one position to the next without shaking, losing your balance, or moving any other part of your body.

5. Try to look relaxed and at ease when you do the motions. You can achieve this if you practice them at a faster-than-normal speed. Try to do the yell as fast as you can without making mistakes or losing uniformity. If you start looking sloppy, slow down again and move faster only when everyone can stay together. If you can do the cheer correctly in unison at high speed, the motions will look relaxed and effortless when done at normal speed. This will result in an appearance of being relaxed even though you are tense and ready to spring to the next motion.

Here are some suggestions to help you build uniformity in your squad. You will find others in Chapter 11.

Arms. To make your arm motions sharp and effective, learn to move them without moving other parts of your body. This means you should be able to stand in place and move your arms quickly from one position to the next without turning your upper body or hunching your shoulders. When you can do this, you will have better balance as well as more uniformity.

The ability to perform motions this way requires a combination of strength and limberness. Practice in front of a mirror and work on learning to move one arm at a time and then both arms together. Here is an arm exercise:

1. Right arm straight up in the air.
2. Right arm straight down at your side.
3. Right arm straight in front of you, palm down.
4. Right arm across chest with bent elbow, palm down.
5. Right arm out to right side, elbow straight, palm down.
6. Right arm straight up, and repeat.

Practice this exercise a number of times rapidly with each arm and then with both arms together.

Your goal is to achieve the ability to move each arm rapidly from one position to the next without any other body movement. The arm goes directly to the new position and stops abruptly; it does not waver or wander. For example, when you swing your arm out to your side, imagine yourself standing with your back against a wall. Your arm swings out and stops sharply as it hits the imaginary wall.

Practice with a mirror and develop a mental picture of where your arms are supposed to be. By developing the ability to feel the type of motion that achieves the position you want, you will be able to duplicate the position at performances.

Uniformity of arm positions is sometimes difficult because there are so many odd angles at which the arms can be placed. Achieving uniformity is easier if parallel lines and right angles are used. If an arm is out to the side, it is parallel to the ground. If it is up, it is parallel with your body and perpendicular to the ground. If one arm is up and the other is out to the side, they form a right angle.

Odd angles and unusual positions are effective for novelty effects but should be used sparingly unless you have lots of rehearsal time.

Hands. If you are using straight arm motions in your routine, keep your wrists straight so that your hands will move in the same way as your arms.

Hold your hand so that you: keep the fingers together, hide the thumb by keeping it beside the fingers, and always show the thin side of your hand to the spectators. For example, when your arms are straight out to the side, keep the palms down or up. When the arms are over the head, turn the palms sideways to the spectators. Go through your cheers ahead of time and decide which way the palms of your hands will face in each position, and then see that each squad member holds his the same way.

When you have your arms down at your sides, point the fingers straight at the ground, but do not press your arms against your sides. When you press your arms against your sides, you appear to be *reaching* down instead of *pointing* down. This position will look better if you bend your elbows slightly.

When using a clenched fist, keep the wrist straight and use a slashing motion with the forearm. When using a hands-on-hips position to start or end a yell, it should look as neat as the other motions and not appear to be merely a position of rest. Most of the spectators will be above you and looking down at you from an angle. This angle tends to make you look shorter and wider than you really are. You can appear taller if you put your hands on the hipbone instead of at the waist. Keep your fingers straight and together. If your wrist is kept straight, you will have a sharp, unbroken line from elbow to fingertips. Keep the thumb tight against the fingers and put the tip of the thumb on the hipbone. Let the fingers extend in front of the hip. When you take your hand off the hip, it will already be in the right position for the next motion.

When you clap, extend your arms well out in front of you and use big, sweeping motions. This is especially important if your squad wears gloves as the spectators can see the beat and not have to listen for it.

Face. When performing, there is just one position for the head—toward the spectators. Even when the body is facing or moving sideways, look over your shoulder at the spectators. This makes uniformity of head position in your squad easy to achieve.

If you say the words of the cheer, your facial expressions will match the yell. Your face will be animated as when talking normally. If you do not say the words, your face will have a blank expression as if you were listening. Avoid arm and hand positions that cover your face. Resist the temptation to look elsewhere during a cheer, such as at nearby players or at someone creating a disturbance. Give the spectators the same attention you expect from them.

Feet and Legs. Because there are fewer positions for the feet and legs, it is easier to achieve uniformity with them than with the arms. The *degree of knee bend* and the *size of steps* are the two things that will have the greatest effect on uniformity of feet and legs. On a lunge, for example, the knee bend should be the same for every member of the squad.

A uniform step is essential for keeping your lines straight. If you start in a straight line, then take a certain number of steps forward, you will end in a straight line *only* if everyone takes the same size step.

When you are not moving, have your feet either close together or well apart. Uniformity can be achieved on feet-apart positions by having the weight of each squad member distributed in the same way. The weight can be more over one foot than the other or it can be evenly distributed.

As with arm motions, big leg motions such as kicks should look easy and effortless. Keep the rest of your body still so that you do not look as if the effort of kicking might knock you off-balance. If the rest of the body is kept still, the squad members only have to concentrate on the matching of leg positions.

11

Teamwork

It is easy to recognize an outstanding performance but sometimes hard to explain exactly why one unit looks better than another. Here is a list of qualities you will find in all outstanding squads. (To rate your own unit, read over the descriptions of each topic and decide where your unit needs work. Following the chart, you will find discussions of each subject. If you have rated your unit in the "needs work" section of a category, you can refer to the appropriate paragraph for suggestions.)

TOPIC	GOOD	NEEDS WORK
Leadership and Signals	The unit starts immediately when the routine is announced or music starts. Each member looks confident and acts like he knows exactly what he is doing.	The squad looks like a group of individuals, all waiting for one another to begin. The group has difficulty getting organized and usually starts its performance after an awkward pause.
Spacing	The unit starts perfectly spaced and stays that way throughout the routine, seemingly without effort.	Individuals are correcting their position before the routine starts. They are obviously moving about

		during the routine to correct spacing errors, or spacing is incorrect and nothing is done about it.
Formations	All formations are geometric and are easily recognized from any angle.	The spectators must try to figure out what the formations are supposed to be, or who is out of place, instead of giving their full attention to enjoying and following the performance.
Precision	All members start motions together, do them the same way and stop them exactly together without having to watch one another.	Motions of some members do not match. Either they do not seem to be doing anything to correct mistakes or their efforts at correction are strained and obvious.
Jumps	Jumps appear to be the same height and done in the same style. Members do not have to watch one another to get organized or to get their motions to match following the jump.	Jumps are not together, are different heights and styles. Some members look a lot better than others. There is confusion following the jump while everyone gets organized for the next position.

HOW TO RAISE YOUR RATING FROM "NEEDS WORK" TO "GOOD"

Every unit will have different problems that require different solutions. You are the best person to judge what is needed to improve your squad; but here are some general ideas you can use as a guide:

Leadership and Signals

Leadership. A successful and organized group will have just one leader. If you have more than one person in your unit who has the ability to be the leader, rotate the job from week to week or have one leader for football, another for basketball. But only one person is leader at any given time. The job is not shared!

The chosen leader must be in charge at rehearsals and performances. He should encourage suggestions and ideas from other members, but his decision is final. If members have something to contribute or a suggestion they think will improve the appearance of the unit, they should make the suggestions at the rehearsals. They should not suggest changes at the game, as it is best not to try anything new until the whole squad has had a chance to practice it.

Good leadership is based on a good working relationship among all members. Before the season starts, the leader should help establish methods of settling differences of opinion. Decide who is in charge of what, who has the final decision on various topics, and what subjects are to be decided upon by a majority vote.

Decide among yourselves that you are going to give as well as take criticism from one another and be good natured about it. Agree that if someone tells another to hurry up or to move over that no offense will be taken. Criticisms of this type are not personal ones but made only for the good of the squad. Be able to criticize one another during rehearsal and still remain good friends.

At the games make only essential criticisms. Save minor ones for the next rehearsal. Squad members should be aware that things happen fast at games. Often there is no time for politeness or to go into details, and, under tension, people sometimes say things they do not really mean.

Cheerleaders should be capable of acting in a more mature way than the average student their age. They should be able to discuss and come to decisions without some members pouting or acting overbearing. Leaders and captains should always give consideration to a criticism or suggestion that is made in an effort to improve the appearance of the entire squad.

Signals. A well-practiced squad needs few signals. They are always alert and are so familiar with the routines that all they need is a word or wave from their leader to take up their positions. Usually, the leader will tell them ahead of time what the next cheer will be. But if the situation requires a change or the leader decides on his next cheer at the last moment, the other cheerleaders can pick it up when the leader announces the yell to the students. When the leader starts his first motion, the others are ready to start with him. A good squad will not need their own starting signal. Once the yell is underway, the squad members have no reason to watch the leader or one another. They have practiced the routine so well that they know perfectly the motions, positions, and timing of the cheer.

Spacing

Good spacing means that your squad keeps a uniform distance between each member. This can be a problem, especially at the first of the season. Additional practice will not always cure it unless the practice follows a definite plan. One way to practice is to mark spots on the floor for each member. They will quickly learn to take their position without having to measure off and move around.

Entrances will need the most work. A squad that has practiced its spacing will automatically line up properly every time and will look sharper than a team that shuffles around until everyone is finally in the starting position. Have someone time your entrances with a stop watch, and do not be satisfied until you can no longer shorten the time it takes for your unit to get into position.

It may help your squad to improve its spacing if you ask each member to think of himself as trying to stay in line with only two other people; those on each side of him. This is easier than trying to line up with the whole squad. Each person should stand halfway between those on each side of him.

Squad members should not have to turn their heads to see

where they are. Practice looking straight ahead at the spectators and watch the persons on each side of you out of the corners of your eyes. This is called "peripheral vision" and all good cheerleading teams use it.

An inexperienced squad member can be spotted quickly because he will be turning his head frequently to see what the others are doing. They usually concentrate first on one side and then the other so that they are constantly moving from one out-of-line position to another. They overcorrect their mistakes and make new ones as a result. A good cheerleader gives the impression he is looking directly at the spectators all during the cheer.

Formations

Some squads start out their routine with good spacing but when they move to a new formation, the spacing becomes incorrect. This can happen even though each person took the same number of steps. Each squad member may have a natural stride of a different length, and some squad members' legs may be shorter than others. So, in addition to planning how many steps you are going to take in the formation change, you must establish a standard size for each step.

Your best bet is to use a short step. A tall person will look natural taking a short step, but the squad will have an awkward appearance if a short person must take a long step.

Once you decide on a standard step, you will find it easier to maintain proper spacing in your formations. When practicing, use something to mark the ground or floor for your old and new positions. Then try going through the routine without looking at the marks. Once you have moved to the new position, stop and check to see how close you came to the new mark.

Do not try to get too fancy with your formations. Keep them simple and easy to recognize, preferably in a basic geometric pattern. Formations should improve the appearance of the performance and not attract adverse attention. If you keep your formations simple, you will learn them quickly and have more time to spend on more important things, such as staying together. If your squad has a complicated formation that it does well, use it in novelty yells or production-type cheers.

The following charts illustrate basic formations using simple geometrical shapes, such as circles, squares, triangles, and vertical, horizontal, and diagonal lines.

FOR THREE MEMBERS

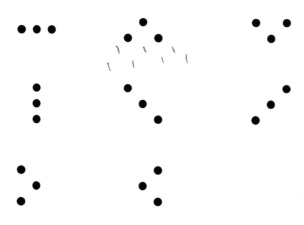

FOR FOUR MEMBERS

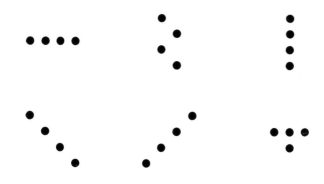

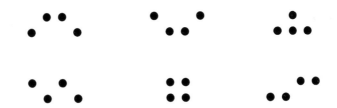

FOR FIVE MEMBERS

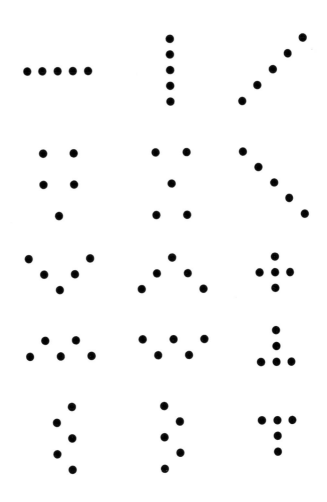

FOR SIX MEMBERS

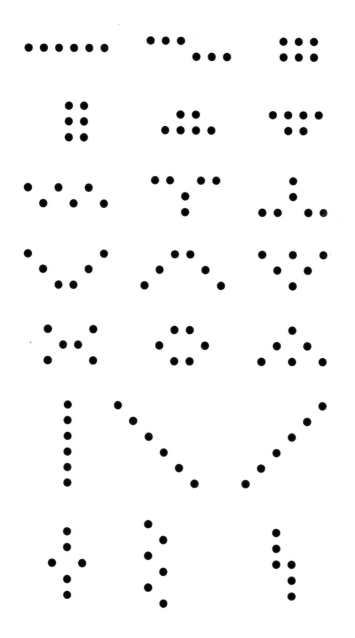

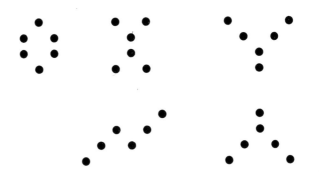

Precision

If your squad is having problems developing precision, check the following four systems used by outstanding squads to achieve precision. You may find that you are doing all of these things but you may not be doing them in the right order or you may be missing one of the steps.

1. Develop a Model of Your Routine. Build it motion by motion with every experienced member contributing ideas and suggestions. The model is completed only when the squad is satisfied with the routine and the members understand the motions and know how they should be done. Have the routine written down as it is created and, if possible, distribute copies to each member. Remember that people will work harder to learn routines that they have helped to create.

2. Give Each Member an Equal Opportunity to Learn the Routine Correctly. Let the squad members take turns standing as close to the leader as possible. The farther you are away from someone you are trying to copy, the harder it is to copy him accurately. If you stand in a long line, rotate so that those on the end have a chance to get an accurate picture of what they are to do.

3. Let Each Member Practice the Routine Individually. Once the members have reached the point where they can go through the whole routine correctly, they should spend some time working on it by themselves. At this time they can work out the exact details and devote extra time to the parts of the routine they need to work on most. A big help in this is a large mirror or picture window in which you can see your reflection as you practice.

4. Rehearse the Squad Together on the Final Details of Precision. If your unit is large, practice first in pairs, then with two pairs together. You will find it easier to learn to stay together in small groups at first. Once you have the whole group together, try practicing again in front of a mirror or picture window. (Most dance studios have large mirrors, if one is not available at your school.)

You can also try the "talking mirror" method where members take turns watching the group and pointing out places where squad members are not doing the same thing. The person watching does not have to know who is right or wrong; he just points out where there is a difference. Once a difference is pointed out, the individual members will be able to make the corrections themselves.

When in doubt, check with the model you established in the beginning. Do not make any changes in the model unless a majority agrees, and then correct the written routine. Without a definite model in writing, you have no way of telling who is right and who is wrong.

After the members do the basic motions of the routine alike, there are a number of other things which you can do to improve your precision. Here is a list of them. (*Note:* If your squad is new or is working out the first routine of the season, spend a long time perfecting the things on this list. They will carry over to all of your other routines, and each new routine will be perfected faster than the previous one.)

1. Keep your head up and look at the spectators. Do not look at your feet or other squad members as you did while learning the routine.

2. Feet are *together* when standing still.

3. On motions where the feet are supposed to be apart, see that everyone has the same distance between his feet.

4. When picking up the feet, everyone raises their knees the same height.

5. Hold the arms out from the body so that the motions will look big.

6. Stand up straight.

7. Fingers are together when the hands are on the hips.

8. For a hands-on-hips position, everyone has their hands at the same level. (You will find it looks better if you put your hands slightly below waist level for this position.)

9. On all extended arm positions, keep the fingers and thumb together.

10. Check your timing on motions. If you have a point that requires special emphasis, see that each member gives it the same amount of emphasis at the same time, without hesitation or anticipation.

11. Check your rhythm on words by having all cheer-leaders say the words aloud when practicing. This will tell you if anyone is slow or jumping the gun on words.

12. Check your spacing to see that everyone is keeping the same distances between them.

13. Do not use the excuse that you cannot get precision because your members are different sizes. If your positions and motions match, the difference in physical sizes will not be so noticeable.

14. If you follow these suggestions and still cannot get good precision, your routine is probably too complicated. Make it simpler. Complicated routines are done well only by experienced teams that have put in plenty of practice. Start easy and make your routines harder as you learn to work together.

Jumps

Good-looking jumps are hard for one person to do and are even more difficult when done by a team. But you will find the extra practice rewarding since good teamwork on jumps is spectacular, and will make your unit stand out.

The secret to jumping together is taking off together. Develop a set preparation that everyone uses. Start together, do the preparation together, and take off together.

Once you start practicing jumps together, you will soon find that some of your squad members can jump higher than others. They will finish their jump after the others. If those who finish first go directly to the next motion without waiting, your precision is lost. There are two ways you can make your jumps look uniform in this situation:

1. Determine the jumping height of your poorest jumper and train everyone to jump just that high and no higher.

2. A better way is to choose a position at the end of the jump that everyone is required to hold, until the best jumper is ready to continue. This lets all the cheerleaders jump to the best of their ability and retains precision without penalizing the better jumpers. You will make all of your jumps look neat and sharp when you follow them with a brief pose, crouch, or lunge.

If you choose the second method, see that everyone does the landing pose the same way. The hands should be in the same position, and the direction of the body and feet should match. While in the pose, you and the students take a deep breath for the next word of the cheer or for shouting if the cheer is finished.

If you have such a wide range of jumping ability in your team that you cannot get precision no matter what you do, use your jumps in spellouts where the members jump one at a time.

If your team wants to do two or three jumps one after the other in a series, set aside extra practice time. To do just one jump together well is hard enough. It is even harder to get precision on a series of team jumps.

TEAM SPIRIT

Let us assume that you have read over this chapter and your squad has worked on the things that will improve your teamwork. You have a sharp-looking squad but you want to be the best in your league. There is one final thing to consider—spirit.

A team with spirit stands out. It has an air of confidence and exuberance in everything it does. The members make maximum efforts look easy. They perform in an inspired way and inspire those who follow them. A team with spirit wants all of their performances to be outstanding. They consider anything less than an outstanding job to be an unsatisfactory one.

Spirit is built up during practice. It is an attitude and feeling that the cheerleaders develop through working together under fair, pleasant, and stimulating conditions.

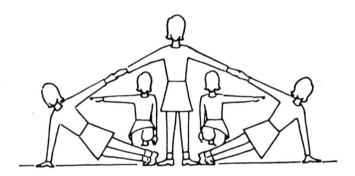

V

For Girls Only

12

Song Leading

How to Be a Success at a Challenging Job

Cheerleading and song leading are separate and distinct activities. Each has a special purpose and those squads that recognize and understand the differences will perform better for their school.

The cheerleaders direct and control the students who participate with them in the yells. The song leaders are primarily entertainers. Song leaders do not lead the songs since the students already know the words. They provide something entertaining, interesting, and peppy to watch while the students are singing.

The jobs of the cheerleaders and the song leaders are both important and, to be done properly, should not be combined. Schools that ask one unit to fill both jobs will usually get a substandard performance in one or the other, no matter how hard the squad tries. If your school has just one squad, talk to your adviser or principal to see if you can get separate teams established.

When the teams are divided, they can specialize in one area rather than try to do both. The individual members will not be under as much pressure and will give better performances. If you can have only one team and are forced to work as a combination cheerleading-song leading squad, spend the greater part of your time on cheerleading.

The desired qualities for song leaders are different from those for cheerleaders. Song leaders should have separate try-outs and be judged on the requirements of their position.

Here are some of the specialized requirements on which a song leader is judged:

1. Ability to learn new dance steps quickly.

2. Ability to memorize the order of the steps in a routine quickly.

3. Gracefulness and ability to make motions look attractive without advice from others.

4. Attractiveness in face and figure. Does she look neat and feminine in appearance and does she radiate youthful good looks and health?

5. Ability to retain her popularity with others even though she has been appointed to a glamorous position.

6. Ability to get along with other girls as attractive, popular, and charming as herself without getting jealous. She does not consider her job as a challenge to get the most attention. The contest was at the tryout. Once she is on the squad, she considers the competition over.

Song leading is approached from a different point of view from cheerleading. However, there are several chapters in this book that contain valuable information that will apply to your job. As you read them over, think how the information can help you as a song leader.

Chapter 2   Your Personal Popularity
Chapter 9   Jump! And Look Good Doing It!
Chapter 11   Teamwork
Chapter 13   Your Uniform

If you are asked to help plan rallies and other school-spirit activities, you will find the chapters in Part III particularly helpful.

HOW SONG LEADERS ATTRACT AND
HOLD STUDENT ATTENTION

Cheerleaders attract the students' attention by talking to them, often over a microphone. Song leaders attract attention by giving an attractive performance. You are helped, of course, by the band. If the students know you are going to present something delightful to watch every time the band plays, they will look forward to your performances and you will have no problem getting their attention.

If you do the same old routines over and over in the same old way and your repertoire does not contain any surprises, you can maintain the attention of the students only by sheer force of your personality. This is only partially effective as it is hard to project your personality all the way to the back of the stands.

If your repertoire is interesting, changed often and you perform well together, the students will get in the habit of looking at you. If, on the other hand, your repertoire is small or you do not have the routines perfected, they will look at you only when they have nothing else to do. This will not be very often as there are lots of interesting things going on at athletic events.

If your student body finds the opponents' song leaders more interesting than you, it will be because the routines are different from those that they are used to seeing. It does not necessarily mean that the other song leaders are any better.

HOW TO KEEP THE STUDENTS INTERESTED

Variety is the key to keeping the students interested in your performances. After they have seen you a few times, they will start looking for something new and different. Here are three easy ways to put variety into your performances:

1. Plan a number of short, distinctive routines rather than a few long or repetitious ones. Do not wear out one particular routine by using it too often. Use different routines as often as possible to keep the students in suspense. If each routine is different from the others and if you rotate them, the students will always look forward to your performances.

2. In a routine you do frequently, certain sections can be changed while keeping the basic idea and the music the same. You might set aside one segment of the routine to be changed from time to time. The change does not have to be complicated in order to be interesting but it must be obvious.

The students do not know the routines as well as you do and they will not notice small changes.

Examples of changes that are easy to make include different starting and ending poses, the use of pyramids, or doing the same motions with a formation change. It will be essentially the same routine done to the same music, but you will have added something to keep the students interested in watching you.

This is especially helpful on the routine you do to the school fight song. The students will probably see this one more than any other. You can use the same routine all through one season and still keep it interesting by changing specific parts of it from time to time.

3. You can make a routine different by changing, adding, or subtracting props. Use umbrellas on a rainy day, a cane on warm ones. Pom poms can be exchanged for pennants or white gloves. The mood of the routine can be changed with different hats, such as sailor hats, big straw hats, top hats, etc.

You can save the old motions, but change the music. The new music should be in the same tempo as the old so that the motions will fit. Your band director will probably be able to suggest new music that will fit the routine.

If the students have become bored with one of your routines, you do not have to throw it away and start over. Simply change the theme and the music. Make a few minor but obvious changes in the arrangement of the routines; add a new beginning and ending and you have a brand-new routine. This can be done with a lot less effort and time than it would take to create a completely new routine.

PUTTING TOGETHER A SUCCESSFUL ROUTINE

Selecting the Music. This should be one of your first considerations. Appropriate music is probably the single most important thing in putting together a successful routine. People like to hear familiar melodies, so select tunes that the students will recognize. And select music that will sound good when played at athletic events.

Not all music sounds good when played by a band. First, think how the music of your choice will sound when played by *any* band; then consider how it will sound when played by *your* band. Your band director can tell you if it is within the capabilities of your band members.

The music the band plays for you is only one of many selections they learn. If you show an understanding of the band's problems, the band director will be more interested in meeting your needs. He may even have some tune suggestions that would be appropriate. Once you make a selection and the band learns it for you, you are expected to use it.

You will find that most popular songs are too long for the time period in which you will perform your routines. Choose songs that will sound good and be recognizable if only a portion is used.

Ask the band director if a tape recording can be made of the band playing the music for your routines. You can then use this tape and practice any time you wish instead of practicing to the music only when the band is rehearsing. Also, it will help you to determine if the music is played the way you want it. If it is not, adjustments can be made before it is used at a performance.

Organizing a Novelty or Specialty Routine. If you are new at putting routines together, here is a suggested format you can use. Not all routines follow this system but it will give you something to start with.

A good basic routine is a series of distinctive, individual ideas. Here are some common elements:

1. Entrance or introduction.
2. Main theme of routine (may include two different sections or types of steps).
3. Change of pace (formation change, special stunt, or novelty step).
4. Return to style of main theme, using different steps or same steps in different formations.
5. Ending.

Once you have put together a tentative arrangement of

your routine, take turns watching the others perform it and ask these questions:

1. Does the beginning attract attention?

2. Is the routine entertaining from beginning to end? Does each section appear distinctive?

3. Is the music played at the right speed for your unit? If the music is too fast, the girls will appear to be hurrying and will be unable to do each motion completely. If some girls are getting ahead of the music, it is too slow. Here is something to remember about speed: more mistakes are usually made at fast speeds than at slow speeds. However, when the music is fast, individual mistakes are not as noticeable as they are when the music is played slow. As you practice, you will discover that there is a certain speed at which your unit looks best. Once you determine this speed, you can choose the speed of music.

4. Is there continuous interest? There should be no "unimportant" parts in your routine. It should not look like you ran out of ideas.

5. Is the routine unique? Does it add variety to your repertoire? Does it look like you have copied ideas from other squads in your league?

6. Is the routine within the capabilities of your members? Can they make it look easy or does it look like they are straining?

7. Does the routine have a highlight or identifying characteristic? If you have a special pose, stunt, or novelty idea in each routine, the students will remember it and watch for the routine again.

8. Does the routine end neatly? Is the ending lively and interesting?

HOW TO PARTICIPATE AS MUCH AS YOU SHOULD

Song leaders can play an important role in building school spirit and in rally activities. If song leading is new at your school or if past song leaders have not taken an active part in school activities, there are many things you can do to increase your own prestige and popularity.

Around School. You can create a special identity for your group with look-alike sports outfits or matching school clothes that you wear occasionally. Do things together, such as planning skits for the rallies in which the song leaders participate as a group, or developing a song-leader act for the talent show. Get your student body in the habit of thinking of you as a distinct group.

At Games. Offer to help the cheerleaders on certain yells, such as novelty cheers, spellouts, and conversation-echo type yells. These work well with a large group leading them. Work out simple steps for the chants. For one-word yells, use single motions or jumps. Use your pom poms for special effects. At the beginning of the game, enter the field ahead of the band or team and run down the track waving the pom poms. When the team scores a touchdown, some squads kneel at the goal line and bow up and down together with their pom poms.

Your main job is to entertain during musical numbers. If your cheerleaders seem cool to the idea when you volunteer to help on cheers, do not force yourselves on them. Leading cheers is their area and they may not want any help. But if they are really sincere about doing a good job for their school, they will invite you to assist them as much as possible. Accept every opportunity offered.

YOUR PUBLIC IMPRESSION

Consider how you look to the spectators during every minute of the game. At any given moment, someone is probably looking at you, even when you are not performing. Think how you appear to the students. Stand or sit attractively and act interested in the game, even if you do not fully understand it. The students will not be fooled if you turn on the charm and enthusiasm only when it is time for your performance.

Stay in a group between performances. When it is time for a routine, go to your position quickly. You have an advantage over the cheerleaders in that most of the time you will know what your next routine will be ahead of time. There is no excuse for failing to start the routine promptly. It is helpful before each game to make up a list of the special novelty routines you plan to use, and go over the list with your band director. He will inform the band members ahead of time so that they will have your music ready. Otherwise, there might be an awkward pause while you are standing ready to go but the band is looking for your music.

Coordinate your routines with your yell captain. When he or she knows ahead of time what you plan to do, you will often get a special announcement or introduction. While performing, look at the students and smile. Look like you enjoy what you are doing. Move your gaze about them. If you just look in one area, the rest of the spectators will think you are ignoring them.

You will not have to worry about your public impression if the girls on your squad are vivacious, popular, and attractive. They are aware of their responsibilities and want to do the best job they can. You have a variety of interesting routines that you perform well. Each squad member gets along with the others, the band director, and the students.

HOW TO MAKE THE MOST OF POM POMS

Try for a feeling of continuous motion in your pom pom routines. Here are some methods for getting motion into a routine to make it interesting even though the speed remains the same:

1. Combine the arm and leg motions in different ways.
   a) Use two or three arm motions for each leg position.
   b) Use several leg motions for each arm position.
   c) Use one arm motion for each leg motion.
2. Use different motions for moving and for standing still.
   a) Use big arm motions when standing in one place.
   b) When moving, use fewer and smaller arm motions and use sweeping motions that carry through several counts of the music.

If you use your imagination, you will find it easy to create a variety of interesting pom pom routines and tricks. Some squads make their routines look different by using pom poms of various sizes and colors, flags, canes, or other props. A simple way to make a routine look new is to change the music.

Pom pom routines can be done in poor weather by using white gloves only, or by making a special set of waterproof pom poms from strips of colored plastic.

Look after your pom poms. Store them in plastic bags to keep them clean and dry. Shake them out vigorously before every game so that you do not litter the area with loose strands. During the game, display them neatly when you are not using them. Do not just scatter them or throw them around.

13

Your Uniform

Most cheerleaders and song leaders either help design their own uniforms or are asked to contribute ideas for them. You are going to be asked for your opinions, and you should have good reasons for your ideas if they are new or different.

Before you present your ideas to others, check them out for yourself against the following six questions about your uniform:

1. Will the students think it is attractive and in good taste?

2. Will your parents and teachers think it appropriate?

3. Will the girls who wear it find it comfortable, easy to maintain, and flattering to their figure and personality?

4. Will it have design features that are easy to duplicate so that each uniform matches *exactly*?

5. Will the uniform minimize differences in height and weight of members and increase the look of uniformity?

6. Will your plan fit the budget? Have you checked out the costs of materials and dressmaking ahead of time so that you have all the facts and figures?

If you can answer "yes" to each of these questions, your ideas have a better chance of success.

In your final selection of materials and style, consider whether the uniform will be worn indoors, outdoors, or both, and how long it must last. To help you in the selection of your uniform, here are some ideas and suggestions from cheerleaders and song leaders that have been presented at camps and clinics:

SUGGESTIONS ON SELECTING MATERIAL

Choose material that will not wrinkle easily. You want to be able to sit down in the uniform without it showing wrinkles when you get up to lead a yell. The material should not fade or stretch out of shape when cleaned.

If you combine two colors in one part of the uniform, such as a two-color pleated skirt, select material that is dye-fast so that the colors will not run into each other. If the material is going to shrink or stretch even the slightest bit, use the same material for both colors so that they will change shape the same amount.

The material should be sturdy enough so that outlines of undergarments do not show through. Select a material that will not cling to every curve when it gets wet. You will not want to send the uniform to the cleaners every time you get a spot on it, so select a material that will not show spot-removing efforts.

SUGGESTIONS ON SELECTING STYLES

The style of your uniform should fit in with your school theme, mascot, or colors. Try to imagine yourself wearing the finished uniform in front of your student body. Will it be appropriate for the situation? Will it be right for the weather and will it be able to stand a lot of vigorous movement? Does it immediately associate you with your school?

If your school colors are difficult to combine attractively or if you cannot find materials in the right color, consider a basic white or black uniform and trim it in your school colors.

If the uniform will be used for night and day games, make the major portion of it a light or bright color. Dark uniforms do not stand out at night. Strong, definite colors hold up better if the uniform has to last a while. Pale, intermediate colors tend to look faded, and dull with age.

Choose a style that is functional. Blouses that come out

and waistlines that travel up and down as you move will detract from your performance. Do not forget the tights. They should be in your plans from the beginning. If you wear skirts that are knee length or shorter, the tights will show many times during your routines.

You have a special problem if your school has a limited budget and you must make one uniform do for both indoor and outdoor events. Try mix-and-match outfits that can be made warmer or cooler as required, or get matching jackets or sweaters to wear over the uniform on cold days.

SUGGESTIONS ON ACCESSORIES

If you plan to use gloves, hair bows, trim on your shoes, or other accessories, give them as much consideration as you would to style and materials. Include them in the plan from the beginning so that your uniform will not look overdone when it is finished. Effective outfits can be spoiled by too many accessories that attract attention to themselves instead of complementing the outfit and the person in it.

The entire squad should discuss hair styles, nail polish, and make up, and be in general agreement. If you appear at the game with extra accessories or an unusual hairdo, the students will think you are trying to hog the show—a quick way to become unpopular. If you appear with less than what you are supposed to have, people will think you either uncooperative or forgetful.

SPORTS OUTFITS

All squads should consider the idea of having one or more sports outfits to wear while traveling to games, at informal school functions, and when attending clinics and camps. This outfit will identify you and the squad on many occasions where you might not otherwise be known as the cheerleaders or song leaders for your school. Sports outfits can vary with styles and fashion and be changed often.

SUMMARY

Effective uniforms are the result of thoughtful discussion with plenty of "planning ahead." An attractive and functional uniform is not necessarily the result of spending a lot of money for materials or a costly dressmaker. You will probably be surprised at the results of substituting planning for dollars.

When you see other cheerleaders with striking outfits, compliment them and ask them about how the uniforms were made. You will be able to pick up a number of helpful ideas this way.